Sovereign Intelligence: The Rise of Open-Source Models

Jack Wilson

Published by Masterworks, 2026.

SOVEREIGN INTELLIGENCE: THE RISE OF OPEN-SOURCE MODELS

First edition. February 20, 2026.

ISBN: 979-8233350443

Written by Jack Wilson.

Also by Jack Wilson

Dull World
Galaxy Outlaws
Blackwood Mountain's Secret: An Oakhaven Dragon Mystery
Sovereign Intelligence: The Rise of Open-Source Models

Sovereign Intelligence: The Rise of Open-Source Models

Sovereign Intelligence: The Rise of Open-Source Models is not merely a technological story but a structural shift in the architecture of power. It begins in an era defined by centralization, where advanced artificial intelligence systems existed behind APIs, wrapped in proprietary access, metered by tokens, and governed by opaque policy layers. Intelligence was rented, not owned. Developers could prompt but not inspect, integrate but not modify, scale but never truly control. Organizations fed data into black boxes and received probabilities in return. The arrangement was efficient, but asymmetrical. It created a dependency loop: innovation flowed upward toward a handful of companies with hyperscale infrastructure, while users adapted their workflows around constraints they could not see. The model weights—the distilled compression of trillions of words, images, and signals—were inaccessible. Intelligence was effectively landlocked.

The emergence of open-weight models changed that geometry. When model weights are released, intelligence becomes portable. It can be downloaded, run locally, modified, fine-tuned, evaluated, and embedded into entirely new systems without permission from a centralized gatekeeper. This shift resembles earlier transitions in computing history: from mainframes to personal computers, from proprietary operating systems to open-source kernels, from controlled publishing networks to decentralized web protocols. Each time code became inspectable and redistributable, creativity expanded and new industries formed. Open-source AI extends that lineage into cognition itself. It suggests that reasoning engines need not be cloud-bound utilities but can become sovereign components of local infrastructure.

The difference between open-source, open-weight, and open-access systems becomes critical in this landscape. Open-access may grant usage through an interface but keeps architecture and weights closed. Open-weight systems release the trained parameters but may restrict training data or commercial use depending on license. Fully open-source projects provide transparency across code, weights, and training pipelines. These distinctions determine whether a system can be audited for bias, modified for domain specialization, optimized for specific hardware, or embedded into regulated workflows. Sovereignty is not binary; it exists on a spectrum defined by transparency, inspectability, and licensing rights. Legal frameworks such as Apache, MIT, GPL, and custom AI community licenses shape how intelligence propagates across industries.

Technically, open models inherit the transformer architecture that defined modern large language models. Attention mechanisms allow tokens to contextualize themselves relative to every other token in a sequence, producing representations that scale across documents, conversations, and multimodal inputs. Training begins with massive pretraining corpora, encoding statistical structure into billions of parameters. Fine-tuning layers then shape behavior through supervised instruction data and reinforcement signals. Alignment processes nudge models toward safety and usefulness. What changes in the open paradigm is not the mathematics but the accessibility. Engineers can now experiment with quantization techniques to compress models into smaller memory footprints. They can deploy on GPUs, edge accelerators, or even optimized consumer hardware. They can build retrieval-augmented architectures where local databases feed context into prompts. They can train adapters or LoRA modules to specialize models without retraining from scratch.

Self-hosting introduces a new operational calculus. Under API-based consumption, costs scale linearly with usage. Under local deployment, capital expenditure replaces per-token billing. Enterprises weigh hardware investment against marginal inference cost. For organizations with sustained workloads, the economic equilibrium often favors ownership. GPUs, inference servers, cooling systems, and orchestration pipelines become upfront infrastructure investments that amortize over time. The total cost of ownership includes electricity, maintenance, DevOps engineering, monitoring, and security hardening. Yet it also includes intangible benefits: data privacy, compliance control, resilience against vendor lock-in, and performance predictability. Sovereign intelligence reframes AI from operational expense to strategic asset.

This transition affects not only enterprises but individuals. Developers can run capable models on workstations. Researchers can audit outputs without external logging. Creators can experiment with customization. Communities collaborate to benchmark, compare, and iterate. Open model leaderboards reveal performance metrics across reasoning, coding, mathematics, and multilingual tasks. Shared fine-tuning datasets accelerate domain-specific adaptation. An ecosystem of tooling grows alongside: model hubs, distributed training libraries, inference engines, orchestration frameworks, and hardware abstraction layers. What was once a monolithic service becomes a composable stack.

The geopolitical implications are equally significant. Nations concerned with digital sovereignty recognize that reliance on foreign cloud infrastructure introduces strategic vulnerability. Open-weight models enable localized AI ecosystems aligned with regulatory norms and cultural context. Universities contribute research without ceding control to multinational providers. Startups differentiate by optimizing open cores rather than reinventing entire foundational stacks. Innovation diversifies geographically.

Within this emerging landscape, various model families have shaped momentum. Meta catalyzed discussion through releases in the LLaMA series, challenging assumptions that frontier-scale systems must remain closed. Mistral AI demonstrated that lean research teams could produce competitive open-weight architectures with strong reasoning and efficiency characteristics. Stability AI extended openness into generative imaging, proving that multimodal creativity could flourish under distributed development. OpenAI, though primarily associated with closed commercial APIs, accelerated the public's understanding of large-scale language modeling and helped define the benchmark environment in which open alternatives would compete. The dialectic between openness and commercial secrecy continues to drive rapid iteration across the ecosystem.

Governance remains complex. Open-source communities thrive on transparency but must also navigate misuse risks, intellectual property concerns, and safety considerations. Releasing weights can enable beneficial innovation while simultaneously lowering barriers for harmful applications. Responsible disclosure practices evolve. Community red-teaming supplements formal evaluation. Researchers debate whether safety alignment improves under centralized stewardship or distributed inspection. Sovereign intelligence does not eliminate these tensions; it redistributes them across broader participation.

Customization is perhaps the most transformative capability unlocked by openness. A hospital can fine-tune a medical reasoning model on anonymized internal records without transmitting sensitive data externally. A law firm can adapt models to jurisdiction-specific precedents. A manufacturing company can embed domain knowledge from proprietary manuals. Through parameter-efficient fine-tuning, these adaptations require relatively small computational overhead compared to training from scratch. Edge deployments integrate language capabilities directly into devices—industrial sensors, robotics controllers, educational tablets—extending intelligence beyond browser windows into physical systems.

The cultural effect mirrors early internet decentralization. Forums, researchers, and independent engineers collaborate across repositories. Novel architectures propagate quickly. Quantized variants appear days after base releases. Optimized inference engines reduce latency. Documentation becomes communal. Knowledge diffuses horizontally rather than vertically. This participatory innovation model accelerates specialization in unexpected directions.

Sovereign intelligence ultimately reframes AI as infrastructure rather than product. It is a shift from subscription mentality to stewardship mentality. The question changes from "Which API do we call?" to "What stack do we own?" Ownership does not imply isolation; hybrid strategies combine local models with external services for tasks that demand scale. But the baseline assumption evolves: intelligence can reside within one's perimeter.

The deeper philosophical implication lies in agency. When model weights are inspectable, intelligence becomes less mystical and more mechanical. Organizations engage not with an oracle but with a toolset that can be audited and shaped. Engineers understand limitations and can iteratively address them. Trust emerges from transparency rather than branding. Communities learn how models fail as well as how they succeed.

As computing progresses toward multimodal fusion—text, image, audio, code, sensor streams—the open model paradigm positions itself as a modular backbone for emergent ecosystems. Distributed data stores feed context pipelines. Secure enclaves protect inference. Federated learning coordinates updates without centralizing sensitive information. Hardware evolves toward specialized accelerators optimized for transformer workloads. The stack becomes layered: foundation model, fine-tuning adapters, retrieval systems, orchestration agents, user interface. Each layer can be independently improved by an open community.

Sovereign Intelligence: The Rise of Open-Source Models tells the story of this rebalancing. It traces how a community once reliant on distant computational monoliths began reclaiming ownership of the most consequential technology of its time. It explores the mathematics of attention and the economics of infrastructure. It examines licenses and governance, GPUs and quantization, regulation and resilience. Above all, it asks a strategic question: in a world where intelligence shapes productivity, culture, and power, who should control the machinery of thought?

The Closed Box Era began quietly, wrapped in convenience. Artificial intelligence appeared not as a machine you installed, not as a system you configured, but as an endpoint. A URL. A key. A request-response loop. You did not download intelligence; you accessed it. You authenticated against it. You paid for it. And in return, you received output that felt almost magical—language generation, classification, reasoning, summarization—delivered at scale through invisible infrastructure. The architecture was elegant from the outside and impenetrable from within. Models lived in distant data centers, spread across continents, replicated behind load balancers and optimized clusters, trained on vast corpora no single user could inspect. The user was separated from the machine not only by physical distance but by abstraction layers that removed visibility into weights, training data, alignment techniques, optimization constraints, and architectural decisions.

Cloud-only AI defined this era. Intelligence resided exclusively within hyperscale infrastructure operated by a small number of organizations with the capital to train and serve frontier models. These systems required enormous compute budgets—thousands of GPUs running in parallel, interconnected by high-bandwidth networking fabrics, cooled by elaborate thermal systems, powered by megawatts of electricity. The cost of entry ensured that only a concentrated group of entities could participate at the highest levels of model development. For everyone else—developers, startups, researchers, enterprises—the model arrived as a service. You did not see tensor operations; you saw tokens. You did not provision clusters; you configured rate limits.

This access model was undeniably powerful. It accelerated adoption. It removed operational complexity. An individual developer could build tools atop sophisticated language models without worrying about distributed training pipelines or inference optimization. A startup could launch with minimal infrastructure expenditure, paying only for the tokens consumed. Enterprises could prototype generative systems rapidly, integrating APIs into workflows with predictable billing mechanisms. The abstraction lowered friction. But abstraction also concealed dependency.

API dependency became structural. Applications were no longer self-contained software artifacts; they were shells around external intelligence. If the upstream provider changed pricing, modified rate limits, altered model behavior, or revoked access, downstream products were affected instantly. Version updates shifted outputs. Subtle adjustments in alignment modified tone and reasoning. Feature deprecations forced architectural rewrites. An application could be technically sound and operationally fragile at the same time, because its reasoning engine existed elsewhere. Reliability was no longer defined solely by code quality but by the policies and uptime of a provider beyond the developer's control.

This dependency extended beyond economics into epistemology. Users trusted outputs they could not audit. They could not examine training corpora. They could not inspect parameter distributions. They could not evaluate architectural modifications. They saw performance metrics and demonstrations but not the internal mechanics. Intelligence became a sealed artifact. Branding stood in for transparency. Trust was constructed through reputation, compliance certifications, and external audits rather than inspectable code and weights. The metaphor shifted from tool ownership to utility subscription: AI as electricity, delivered through a grid controlled by a handful of operators.

Data control versus user control became one of the defining tensions of the period. When prompts, documents, and proprietary datasets flowed into cloud endpoints, questions emerged about retention, usage, storage, and secondary training. Providers published policies about anonymization and opt-outs, but for organizations in regulated industries, uncertainty remained. Financial institutions worried about confidential records. Healthcare systems worried about patient privacy. Governments worried about jurisdictional boundaries. Sending sensitive data beyond the organizational perimeter introduced risk vectors that compliance teams struggled to quantify. The promise of productivity collided with the need for sovereignty.

Even when providers offered enterprise tiers with enhanced data guarantees, the asymmetry persisted. The provider owned the infrastructure, the model weights, the upgrade schedule, and often the feedback loops that refined the system over time. The user supplied prompts and occasionally reinforcement signals, but rarely shaped the underlying architecture. Control resided where the compute resided. The question was not whether the systems were useful—they demonstrably were—but who ultimately steered their evolution.

The cost structure of centralized intelligence further defined the era. API billing models tied expense directly to usage. At low scale, this was remarkably attractive. There was no need to purchase GPUs or manage clusters. The marginal cost of experimentation was small. But at higher volumes, token-based billing accumulated quickly. Enterprises running sustained workloads found themselves balancing innovation against metered consumption. Each query had a price. Each generation carried a micro-cost that multiplied across thousands or millions of interactions. Forecasting AI expenditure became a new financial discipline within technology organizations.

Beyond direct billing, there was strategic cost: vendor lock-in. Applications deeply integrated with specific APIs faced switching friction. Differences in prompt formats, safety policies, and latency profiles complicated migration. Even if alternative models existed, rewriting integrations and revalidating behavior required engineering resources. This inertia reinforced centralization. The dominant providers benefited not only from scale advantages but from the gravitational pull of ecosystem dependence.

Centralization also influenced innovation pathways. When model training was confined to a few hyperscale labs, research visibility narrowed. Independent researchers relied on published papers and benchmark releases, but could not replicate experiments at equal scale. Open scientific culture adapted by focusing on smaller architectures or theoretical contributions, while frontier-scale experimentation remained largely inaccessible. The gap between public research and private capability widened. Breakthroughs emerged from organizations capable of mobilizing enormous compute budgets, reinforcing the concentration of technical authority.

At the same time, centralized control allowed rapid safety iteration. Providers could deploy alignment updates globally in hours. They could monitor abuse patterns, throttle suspicious activity, and implement policy guardrails consistently. The same infrastructure that enforced dependence also enabled coordinated governance. Whether this was viewed as a benefit or a constraint depended on perspective. For some, centralized oversight meant responsible stewardship. For others, it represented unilateral control over the boundaries of permissible computation.

The Closed Box Era was not malicious in design; it was a consequence of scale economics. Training frontier models demanded resources beyond the reach of most actors. Cloud architectures were optimized for elasticity and global delivery. The API abstraction was efficient. Yet structural efficiency can generate structural imbalance. As AI integrated deeper into education, media, legal analysis, software development, and strategic decision-making, reliance on distant providers acquired geopolitical weight. Nations without domestic access to frontier-scale infrastructure faced reliance on foreign platforms. Digital dependence mirrored earlier dependencies in energy and telecommunications.

Psychologically, the era shaped how society perceived intelligence. AI felt distant and corporate. Users interacted through chat windows, unaware of the hardware layers beneath. The model was a brand, not a machine. Intelligence was something accessed rather than owned. This framing influenced expectations: upgrades arrived as announcements, not as community patches. Transparency was negotiated rather than assumed. The box remained closed because opening it appeared impractical at the highest scales.

Over time, however, friction accumulated. Enterprises calculated escalating token expenses. Developers questioned behavioral drift. Researchers sought greater experimental freedom. Policymakers debated data jurisdiction. The concentration that once seemed inevitable began to appear negotiable. Hardware improved. Distributed training techniques matured. Model compression and quantization reduced inference requirements. The very forces that enabled centralized intelligence—massive data, scalable architectures, powerful accelerators—also laid groundwork for diffusion. What began as a closed system hinted at the possibility of replication.

The Closed Box Era represents a pivotal chapter in the history of artificial intelligence not because it failed, but because it succeeded so thoroughly that its limitations became visible. It proved that large-scale language and multimodal models could transform productivity and communication. It demonstrated that APIs could abstract immense complexity into accessible interfaces. But it also illuminated the trade-offs of dependency, opacity, and centralized cost structures. In doing so, it set the stage for a counter-movement—an exploration of whether intelligence could be distributed, inspectable, and ultimately sovereign.

The case for sovereignty in artificial intelligence emerges from a simple but profound question: who controls the machinery of cognition that now shapes work, communication, strategy, and culture? When intelligence becomes infrastructure, dependence becomes risk. Sovereignty is not an ideological stance against collaboration or cloud innovation; it is a structural assertion that the capacity to reason, generate, and decide should not reside exclusively outside the boundaries of the organization or individual who relies on it. In earlier computing epochs, businesses eventually learned that owning critical infrastructure—networks, servers, databases—provided resilience and strategic flexibility. The same logic now extends to AI systems.

Self-hosting represents digital independence at the architectural level. To self-host an AI model is to bring inference and, in some cases, fine-tuning directly within one's computational perimeter. The hardware may sit in a private data center, a regional facility, or even an on-premise server room, but the defining characteristic is control. The organization decides when models are updated, how they are modified, which data they ingest, how logs are stored, and how outputs are audited. There is no upstream API shaping behavior through remote configuration changes. There is no rate limit imposed by a third-party dashboard. The model becomes a component of internal infrastructure, governed by internal policies.

Digital independence reduces fragility. When mission-critical workflows depend on external endpoints, every outage, policy shift, or pricing adjustment cascades downstream. By contrast, self-hosted systems, while still subject to hardware failure or software bugs, operate within a domain the organization can directly manage. Engineers can optimize performance for specific workloads, deploy redundancy strategies aligned with internal uptime requirements, and integrate AI tightly with proprietary systems. Sovereignty transforms AI from leased functionality into embedded capability.

Data privacy becomes one of the strongest drivers of this shift. In regulated industries such as healthcare, finance, defense, and legal services, information sensitivity is not theoretical. Patient records, trading strategies, classified materials, and confidential contracts represent assets whose exposure carries financial, legal, and ethical consequences. Routing such data through external cloud models introduces compliance complexity. Even with contractual assurances, the act of transmitting data outside the organization creates jurisdictional and auditing challenges. Self-hosted models reduce this exposure by processing sensitive inputs entirely within controlled environments. Logs remain internal. Data retention policies align with local governance standards.

Encryption protocols are defined by the organization rather than inherited from an external service.

Regulatory autonomy extends beyond privacy into adaptability. Different jurisdictions impose distinct requirements around data residency, algorithmic transparency, and risk assessment. A centrally hosted AI service may standardize policies globally, but organizations operating across borders often require localized compliance strategies. Sovereign AI deployments allow model behavior and documentation to be tailored to specific regulatory contexts. If new legislation mandates explainability documentation or model auditing, internally hosted systems can be instrumented and evaluated with granular access to parameters and inference logs. The organization is not dependent on external certification timelines or opaque compliance statements.

The economic case for sovereignty centers on total cost of ownership. API-based AI services typically offer low friction entry. Developers can integrate capabilities within hours. The financial barrier to experimentation is minimal because usage is metered rather than front-loaded. For startups and exploratory teams, this is invaluable. But as usage scales, the cost profile changes. Per-token billing accumulates across thousands or millions of daily interactions. Marginal usage costs persist indefinitely. In high-throughput environments—customer service automation, document processing pipelines, software code generation assistants—the variable cost structure begins to dominate operating expenses.

Total cost of ownership reframes this dynamic by comparing operational expenditure against capital expenditure. Under an API model, expense scales linearly with workload. The more intelligence you consume, the more you pay. Under a local deployment model, significant hardware investment occurs upfront. GPUs or specialized accelerators must be purchased or leased. Servers require cooling, power management, networking infrastructure, and maintenance. Engineering teams must manage deployment pipelines and monitoring systems. These initial costs can be substantial. However, once infrastructure is in place, the marginal cost of inference decreases dramatically. Running one thousand inferences may consume slightly more electricity than running one hundred, but the incremental expense approaches near-zero relative to per-token billing.

For enterprises with predictable and sustained AI workloads, this shift in cost structure can be decisive. Capital expenditure amortizes over time, while operational expenditure compounds. A locally hosted model serving millions of inferences per day may, after the initial investment, deliver outputs at a fraction of the per-token equivalent cost. The breakeven point depends on workload intensity, hardware efficiency, and model optimization, but the principle remains consistent: high utilization favors ownership. This economic reality validates the sovereignty argument not only philosophically but financially.

Cost efficiency differs from scale efficiency. Hyperscale cloud providers benefit from economies of scale in training frontier models and distributing updates globally. They optimize hardware utilization across vast client bases. However, their scale efficiency does not necessarily translate into cost efficiency for every enterprise customer. An organization running domain-specific workloads may not require frontier-scale reasoning across every query. A tuned open-weight model, optimized locally and aligned with specific data patterns, may deliver sufficient performance at significantly lower cost. Sovereignty allows optimization for purpose rather than adherence to generalized capabilities.

Open weights are essential to this equation. Without access to model parameters, self-hosting reduces to mere caching of remote services. True sovereignty requires inspectable and modifiable models. Open-weight releases enable organizations to download the computational heart of the system—the billions of parameters encoding learned statistical structure—and deploy them within their own stacks. They can fine-tune these weights on proprietary datasets, enhancing domain specificity without retraining from scratch. They can quantize models to fit constrained hardware environments. They can integrate retrieval augmentation with internal databases. They can evaluate bias and performance through direct measurement rather than inference.

Control over weights also means control over trajectory. If a cloud provider decides to deprecate a model version, dependent applications must migrate. If safety policies shift, outputs change. With open weights, versioning becomes internal. Updates occur on chosen schedules. Experimental branches can be tested without affecting production systems. Intelligence evolves alongside organizational strategy rather than external roadmaps.

The sovereignty argument is not absolute; hybrid architectures will persist. Organizations may combine local models for sensitive tasks with cloud-based frontier models for broader reasoning challenges. But the presence of open weights makes this hybrid balance possible. Without them, all roads lead outward. With them, strategic choice becomes real.

At its core, the case for sovereignty is about alignment between infrastructure and identity. An organization's AI systems increasingly shape how it communicates, analyzes, and innovates. When those systems are external utilities, control is partial. When they are internal assets, intelligence becomes part of institutional capability. The calculus shifts from subscription management to infrastructure design. Total cost of ownership becomes not merely a financial metric but a measure of independence. As AI continues to permeate core operations, enterprises must decide whether intelligence remains rented bandwidth or becomes owned capital.

What "open" really means in the context of artificial intelligence is more nuanced than the word suggests. In common conversation, "open" implies transparency, accessibility, and freedom. In practice, the term spans a spectrum of technical, legal, and philosophical commitments. To understand the implications of openness in AI, one must distinguish between open-source, open-weight, and open-access systems, because each represents a different distribution of control, visibility, and rights. The distinctions matter not only to engineers but to enterprises, policymakers, researchers, and communities shaping the future of intelligent systems.

Open-access systems are the most common and the most misunderstood. An open-access model allows users to interact with a system, typically through an API or web interface, but does not grant visibility into its inner workings. The architecture, training data, parameter weights, and alignment processes remain proprietary. Users receive outputs, sometimes with documentation and usage guarantees, yet the system itself remains a black box. Open-access lowers barriers to use but does not distribute ownership. It is open in the sense of availability, not inspectability. From a product standpoint, this model enables broad adoption while preserving centralized control. From a sovereignty standpoint, it offers capability without transparency.

Open-weight systems mark a significant shift. In this model, the trained parameters of the neural network—the numerical weights that encode learned representations—are released publicly or semi-publicly. Anyone with adequate hardware can download the model and run inference locally. This move transfers computational agency outward. However, open-weight does not necessarily mean the entire training pipeline is disclosed. The training data may remain private. The preprocessing steps, filtering criteria, or alignment methodologies might not be fully documented. In some cases, the license attached to the weights restricts certain forms of commercial use or prohibits deployment at scale without permission. Open-weight increases inspectability and deployability but may still contain legal or practical boundaries.

Open-source represents the most comprehensive form of openness. In a fully open-source AI project, not only are the weights released, but the source code governing architecture, training scripts, evaluation benchmarks, and deployment mechanisms is also available under a recognized open-source license. Ideally, documentation explains how to reproduce training or fine-tuning processes, enabling replication and modification. The model becomes a communal artifact. Researchers can study architectural decisions. Developers can optimize inference engines. Enterprises can embed systems into products without ambiguity about licensing. Open-source extends beyond distribution; it invites participation.

The differences among these categories are not semantic—they define economic and strategic possibilities. A startup building a product atop an open-access API inherits dependency on pricing models and policy decisions beyond its control. The same startup using open weights may host its own instance and fine-tune for niche domains, reducing cost volatility and customizing behavior. A community building on an open-source project can fork the codebase, propose architectural improvements, or tailor versions for specific hardware environments. Openness determines whether AI is consumed, adapted, or co-created.

Licenses formalize these distinctions. An AI model's license specifies what users can and cannot do with the released artifacts. Permissive licenses such as MIT or Apache allow commercial use, modification, and redistribution with minimal restrictions, fostering broad ecosystem growth. Copyleft licenses like GPL require derivative works to remain open, ensuring that improvements flow back into the community. Some AI-specific licenses introduce hybrid structures, permitting research and limited commercial activity while restricting large-scale competitive deployment. These custom licenses reflect tension between encouraging innovation and preventing exploitation by larger entities.

Commercial implications flow directly from licensing choices. Enterprises evaluating open models must assess not only technical performance but legal compatibility with their business objectives. A permissively licensed model can be integrated into proprietary products without mandatory disclosure of derivative code. A restrictive license might limit revenue-generating deployment or impose reporting requirements. Strategic planning therefore intersects with legal interpretation. Openness does not eliminate governance; it redefines it through codified agreements rather than exclusive ownership.

Licensing also influences competition. When permissive open-source models reach high performance thresholds, they lower barriers to entry across industries. Smaller organizations can build sophisticated products without negotiating expensive API contracts. This democratization can accelerate innovation but may compress margins for incumbent providers. Conversely, when licenses impose scale-based restrictions, they preserve commercial advantage for originators while still allowing research access. The structure of openness becomes a strategic lever shaping market dynamics.

Beyond formal licenses, community governance models determine how open AI evolves over time. Traditional open-source software communities often rely on maintainers, steering committees, and transparent contribution processes. Contributors propose changes through pull requests. Discussions occur publicly. Roadmaps reflect collaborative debate. In AI, governance extends beyond code changes to include considerations of safety, misuse, and ethical deployment. Open communities must establish norms around responsible release, red-teaming, dataset transparency, and vulnerability disclosure.

Some projects adopt foundation-based governance structures, where a non-profit entity oversees development to prevent domination by any single corporation. Others operate under corporate stewardship but allow public contributions. In decentralized ecosystems, multiple forks of a model may emerge, each pursuing distinct priorities—performance optimization, safety hardening, hardware efficiency, or domain specialization. Governance becomes evolutionary rather than hierarchical. Competing visions can coexist within the same architectural lineage.

Community governance also shapes trust. Transparent development processes allow researchers to inspect proposed modifications and assess risk. Public benchmarking promotes accountability. When biases or vulnerabilities are discovered, community members can propose patches. Distributed oversight may reduce reliance on opaque safety claims issued by centralized providers. However, openness does not automatically guarantee responsible behavior. Governance structures must balance freedom with safeguards to prevent malicious exploitation. The tension between accessibility and risk mitigation remains central to the open AI conversation.

Openness intersects with cultural philosophy as well. In earlier computing eras, open-source movements emerged from a belief that software should be inspectable and modifiable by those who rely on it. This ethos emphasized autonomy, collaboration, and shared progress. AI extends this ethos into cognitive infrastructure. When models influence social discourse, business decisions, and creative expression, transparency acquires societal importance. The question becomes not only who can use intelligence, but who can examine and shape it.

At the same time, openness exists within practical constraints. Training frontier-scale models still demands immense computational resources. Full reproducibility may be technically prohibitive for smaller teams. Datasets may contain copyrighted or sensitive material that cannot be redistributed. Thus, the ideal of complete openness often encounters legal and economic barriers. Hybrid forms proliferate. Partial dataset documentation accompanies open weights. Model cards describe limitations. Governance evolves incrementally.

Understanding what "open" really means requires moving beyond slogans. It requires examining the layers of availability, inspectability, modifiability, and legal permissibility embedded in each release. It requires analyzing license clauses and contribution policies with the same seriousness as architectural benchmarks. Openness is not binary. It is multidimensional, encompassing technical access, legal rights, community norms, and strategic intent.

As artificial intelligence becomes foundational to digital infrastructure, these distinctions grow increasingly consequential. Whether intelligence remains concentrated within proprietary silos or diffuses through open ecosystems will shape innovation patterns, economic opportunity, and democratic oversight. The vocabulary of openness is therefore more than descriptive; it is strategic. It defines the contours of participation in the next era of computation.

A large language model is, at its core, a statistical engine designed to predict the next token in a sequence. That deceptively simple objective—next-token prediction—produces behavior that appears to reason, summarize, translate, code, and converse. An LLM does not possess intention or awareness; it operates by transforming input text into numerical representations and computing probability distributions over possible continuations. Yet when trained at sufficient scale on diverse datasets, this probabilistic mechanism yields emergent capabilities that feel qualitatively different from earlier language systems. The shift from rule-based NLP to large-scale generative modeling represents not merely incremental progress but a redefinition of how machines process language.

The foundation of modern LLMs is the transformer architecture. Introduced in 2017, the transformer replaced recurrent and convolutional sequence models with an attention-based structure capable of modeling long-range dependencies in parallel. Instead of processing tokens sequentially like a recurrent neural network, the transformer evaluates relationships among all tokens in a sequence simultaneously through self-attention mechanisms. Each token is represented as a vector embedding, a high-dimensional numerical encoding capturing semantic and syntactic information. Through layers of attention and feed-forward networks, these embeddings are iteratively refined.

Self-attention is the architectural breakthrough that made scaling feasible. For each token, the model computes query, key, and value vectors. Attention weights are calculated by comparing queries to keys across the sequence, determining how strongly each token should attend to others. These weights are normalized and applied to the value vectors, producing context-sensitive representations. In effect, every word in a sentence learns which other words matter most for understanding its meaning in that specific context. Multiple attention heads operate in parallel, capturing different patterns—syntactic relationships, semantic themes, positional dependencies—within the same layer. Stacked across dozens or even hundreds of layers, this process yields increasingly abstract representations of text.

Training an LLM involves exposing this architecture to vast corpora of tokenized data. Raw text is first converted into tokens—subword units derived from algorithms like byte-pair encoding or sentencepiece. Tokenization balances vocabulary size with flexibility, enabling the model to handle rare words and multilingual inputs efficiently. Once tokenized, text sequences are fed into the transformer, and the model learns by minimizing cross-entropy loss between its predicted token probabilities and the actual next tokens in the dataset. Every training step slightly adjusts the model's parameters—the numerical weights connecting neurons—through backpropagation and gradient descent.

Datasets are critical to capability. Modern LLMs are trained on mixtures of publicly available web text, licensed material, curated datasets, books, code repositories, academic articles, and sometimes domain-specific corpora. The diversity and quality of these datasets influence not only linguistic fluency but reasoning patterns, factual coverage, and stylistic versatility. Data preprocessing often includes filtering for duplicates, removing low-quality content, balancing language representation, and eliminating harmful or biased material. Yet the sheer scale—often trillions of tokens—means that statistical regularities dominate.

Compute is the invisible engine powering training. Large models require thousands of GPUs or specialized accelerators running for weeks or months. Distributed training frameworks split models across devices, synchronize gradients efficiently, and manage memory constraints. Training involves billions of forward and backward passes through the network. Each parameter adjustment consumes energy and hardware bandwidth. The cost of training frontier-scale models can reach tens or hundreds of millions of dollars in compute alone, creating economic barriers that shape who can build such systems.

Parameters represent the model's learned knowledge encoded numerically. A parameter is essentially a weight in the neural network—a floating-point number adjusted during training. Early language models contained millions of parameters; modern frontier systems contain hundreds of billions or even trillions. Parameters determine how strongly signals propagate between neurons. During training, the model tunes these weights to capture complex patterns in language. The parameter count correlates with capacity: more parameters allow the model to store and represent more nuanced patterns, though they also increase computational cost.

Scaling laws describe predictable relationships observed in large model training. Empirical research has shown that performance improves smoothly with increases in model size, dataset size, and compute, following power-law trends. Doubling parameters or training tokens often yields incremental yet measurable improvements in loss and downstream task accuracy. These scaling laws provided the conceptual foundation for the rapid growth of model sizes in recent years. They suggested that capability expansion was not random but systematic. If compute and data increased, performance would reliably improve.

However, scaling is not unlimited. Diminishing returns eventually appear if data quality or diversity fails to keep pace. Training efficiency constraints arise from hardware memory limits and energy costs. Researchers experiment with mixture-of-experts architectures, sparse attention patterns, and parameter-efficient fine-tuning to extend scaling benefits without proportional cost increases. The interplay between parameters, tokens, and compute defines the frontier of capability.

Inference differs fundamentally from training. During training, the model adjusts parameters by processing labeled examples and computing gradients. This stage is computationally intensive and requires backward propagation through the network. Inference, by contrast, uses a fixed set of learned parameters to generate outputs in response to new inputs. It involves only forward passes through the network. While still computationally expensive for large models, inference is orders of magnitude cheaper than training because it does not update weights.

During inference, the model receives a prompt—a sequence of tokens—and computes probability distributions over possible next tokens. A decoding strategy then selects tokens sequentially. Greedy decoding picks the highest-probability token at each step. Sampling methods such as temperature scaling or nucleus sampling introduce controlled randomness to produce more varied outputs. Beam search explores multiple candidate sequences to optimize likelihood. Each choice affects output diversity and determinism.

Fine-tuning and alignment processes occur after initial pretraining. Supervised fine-tuning exposes the model to curated instruction-following data. Reinforcement learning from human feedback adjusts outputs toward preferred behaviors by optimizing reward models derived from human evaluations. These additional phases influence tone, safety boundaries, and task adherence. Even so, the core capability arises from pretraining at scale.

An LLM can be understood as a layered probability machine, mapping sequences to continuations via high-dimensional linear algebra. Yet the emergent phenomena—reasoning steps, analogical thinking, code synthesis—appear qualitatively richer than next-token prediction suggests. Researchers debate whether these behaviors reflect implicit world models embedded in parameters or sophisticated pattern interpolation across training distributions. Regardless of interpretation, the mechanism remains grounded in statistical optimization.

The distinction between training and inference has strategic implications. Training concentrates power among those who can afford large-scale compute. Inference democratizes capability once weights are distributed. Parameter-efficient fine-tuning techniques further blur the boundary by enabling customization without retraining entire models. As hardware evolves and architectures optimize, inference may become increasingly local, while training remains centralized or semi-distributed across research consortia.

Understanding what an LLM is requires demystifying both mathematics and mythology. It is neither a conscious entity nor a mere autocomplete system in the simplistic sense. It is a high-capacity function approximator trained to minimize error across massive text corpora, implemented through transformer layers optimized at scale. Its intelligence is emergent, statistical, and constrained by data and objective functions. Yet within those constraints lies transformative capability, reshaping communication, software development, research, and creative expression.

Hardware and infrastructure define the practical boundaries of sovereign intelligence. While large language models are mathematical constructs, their usability depends entirely on the physical systems that execute them. The distinction between GPU and CPU inference is foundational. CPUs are versatile and widely available, but they are not optimized for the dense matrix multiplications that dominate transformer workloads. GPUs, by contrast, are built for parallel computation, capable of executing thousands of simultaneous operations across tensor cores. For large models, GPU acceleration is the difference between sluggish experimentation and real-time interaction. Modern inference frameworks are optimized specifically for GPU execution, leveraging CUDA,

ROCm, or similar acceleration stacks to push throughput and reduce latency.

Video memory, or VRAM, becomes the primary bottleneck for hosting large models. Unlike system RAM, VRAM resides directly on the GPU and determines how much of a model can be loaded for inference. Model parameters occupy memory proportionally to their precision. A 70-billion-parameter model stored in 16-bit precision requires roughly 140 gigabytes of VRAM, placing it far beyond the reach of typical consumer hardware. This is where quantization changes everything.

Quantization reduces the precision of model weights from 16-bit floating-point representations to 8-bit, 4-bit, or even lower numerical formats. By compressing parameter representations, quantization dramatically reduces VRAM requirements while preserving much of the model's capability. Techniques such as GGUF, EXL2, and AWQ enable efficient storage and execution of compressed models. A 70B model that once demanded enterprise-grade hardware can, through 4-bit quantization, operate across two consumer RTX 3090 GPUs. This compression is the technical breakthrough that democratizes deployment. Without it, sovereign intelligence would remain theoretical for most individuals.

Quantization is not merely compression; it is optimization tailored to inference workloads. Advanced schemes selectively preserve higher precision in sensitive layers while compressing others more aggressively, balancing performance and memory efficiency. The result is a practical path to running powerful models in home labs, small offices, or research environments without cloud dependency.

Edge versus cloud deployments reflect strategic architectural decisions. Cloud environments provide elasticity and centralized management, ideal for scaling unpredictable workloads. Edge deployments prioritize locality and privacy, running models directly on devices or within private networks. Sovereign intelligence often favors edge or hybrid designs, especially where data sensitivity or latency constraints are paramount. Running inference locally eliminates round-trip network delays and reduces exposure of confidential information.

A home lab setup represents the grassroots embodiment of this movement. Enthusiasts assemble workstations equipped with high-memory GPUs, robust cooling systems, sufficient power supplies, and fast NVMe storage. Linux-based environments are common, though Windows systems remain viable. Lightweight inference engines load quantized models directly into VRAM. The system may also include local vector databases for retrieval augmentation, allowing the model to reference personal knowledge bases. Through careful hardware selection and software optimization, individuals achieve capabilities once restricted to data centers.

Hardware realities anchor the philosophical case for sovereignty. GPUs provide computational muscle, VRAM defines capacity, and quantization unlocks feasibility. Together, they transform open-weight releases from abstract artifacts into living systems that anyone with the right configuration can run. In doing so, infrastructure ceases to be an invisible dependency and becomes an owned foundation.

Fine-tuning and customization are the mechanisms that transform a general-purpose language model into a specialized system aligned with a specific individual, organization, or domain. A base large language model is trained on vast and diverse corpora, absorbing statistical patterns across languages, disciplines, and formats. While this breadth grants versatility, it does not guarantee precision in specialized contexts. Enterprises require models that understand proprietary terminology, internal documentation structures, product specifications, regulatory language, or institutional tone. Fine-tuning bridges the gap between general intelligence and contextual intelligence.

Traditional full fine-tuning involves continuing the training process on a targeted dataset and updating all model parameters. While effective, this approach is computationally expensive and memory-intensive, especially for models with tens of billions of parameters. Updating every weight demands substantial GPU resources and storage capacity. For most individuals and even many organizations, full fine-tuning of large frontier models is impractical. This constraint led to the development of parameter-efficient techniques that adjust only a small fraction of weights while preserving the bulk of the pretrained model.

LoRA, or Low-Rank Adaptation, represents one of the most influential of these techniques. Instead of modifying the entire parameter set, LoRA injects small trainable matrices into specific layers of the transformer architecture. These low-rank matrices learn task-specific adjustments without overwriting the original weights. The base model remains frozen, and the LoRA adapters encode the customization. This drastically reduces memory requirements and training time while allowing multiple fine-tuned adapters to coexist. An organization can maintain different LoRA modules for legal analysis, marketing copy, or technical documentation, swapping them as needed without duplicating the full model.

QLoRA extends this concept further by combining quantization with low-rank adaptation. In QLoRA workflows, the base model is quantized—often to 4-bit precision—to reduce memory footprint, while the LoRA adapters are trained in higher precision to preserve learning stability. This hybrid approach enables fine-tuning of extremely large models on consumer-grade GPUs. What once required specialized clusters can now occur on high-end workstations. QLoRA effectively lowers the hardware barrier for domain-specific customization, strengthening the feasibility of sovereign AI deployments.

Instruction tuning represents another pivotal layer of refinement. After pretraining, models may exhibit strong language modeling ability but lack consistent task adherence or conversational alignment. Instruction tuning exposes the model to curated prompt-response pairs designed to teach it how to follow directives clearly and predictably. These datasets often include multi-step reasoning, polite refusals, formatting conventions, and structured outputs. The process shapes the model's behavior, making it more helpful and less prone to irrelevant continuation. Instruction tuning shifts a model from pure completion mode to assistant mode, preparing it for deployment in human-facing workflows.

Domain adaptation focuses on embedding specialized knowledge and stylistic norms into the model. A medical institution might fine-tune on anonymized case studies to improve diagnostic reasoning tone. A software company might adapt models using internal code repositories to enhance familiarity with proprietary APIs. Financial firms could align models with regulatory filings, enabling more precise summarization and analysis. Domain adaptation ensures that language patterns reflect real-world application contexts rather than generic web data distributions.

Retrieval-Augmented Generation, or RAG, offers a complementary strategy to fine-tuning. Instead of modifying the model's parameters, RAG integrates external knowledge sources into the inference pipeline. When a user submits a query, the system retrieves relevant documents from a vector database based on semantic similarity. These documents are then inserted into the model's context window, guiding generation. RAG minimizes the need to encode all knowledge inside parameters, reducing hallucination risk and enabling dynamic updates. If the underlying documents change, the system's behavior updates automatically without retraining.

RAG architectures often combine embedding models, vector search engines, and generation models into a coordinated workflow. Documents are chunked, embedded into high-dimensional vectors, and stored in searchable indices. Queries undergo the same embedding process, allowing similarity comparisons. Retrieved passages become contextual scaffolding. This design decouples knowledge storage from reasoning capacity, allowing organizations to maintain real-time synchronization with evolving information sources.

Fine-tuning and RAG are not mutually exclusive. Hybrid systems frequently combine both. LoRA adapters may encode stylistic or domain preferences, while RAG feeds current documentation into prompts. Instruction tuning shapes behavioral norms, while retrieval pipelines supply factual grounding. Together, they enable a layered approach to customization.

What makes these techniques transformative is their efficiency. Parameter-efficient fine-tuning reduces compute demands, quantization minimizes hardware barriers, and retrieval systems externalize memory. These methods empower smaller teams to achieve tailored intelligence without reconstructing models from scratch. Customization becomes a modular exercise rather than a monolithic training endeavor.

In sovereign deployments, fine-tuning represents agency. It allows organizations to shape their systems according to mission and policy. It ensures that intelligence reflects context rather than generic assumptions. And by reducing reliance on centralized providers for every behavioral modification, it reinforces the principle that advanced AI can be adapted locally. Fine-tuning and customization thus complete the loop between foundation model capability and practical utility, turning raw computational power into strategic alignment.

Mistral and its Mixtral line represent a pivotal moment in the evolution of open-weight models, particularly within the European AI ecosystem. At a time when frontier-scale development appeared concentrated within a handful of American and Chinese hyperscale organizations, Mistral demonstrated that a focused research team operating within Europe could produce models that were not only competitive, but architecturally innovative. Their contribution is not merely symbolic; it reshaped assumptions about computational efficiency and structural design in large language models.

The core breakthrough associated with Mixtral is its implementation of a Mixture of Experts architecture. Traditional dense transformer models activate all parameters for every token processed during inference. If a model contains tens of billions of parameters, each token flows through the full computational graph. While this density simplifies scaling logic, it is computationally wasteful. Every parameter participates in every forward pass, regardless of whether it meaningfully contributes to the output in that specific context. This architecture scales performance predictably, but at enormous cost.

Mixture of Experts changes this equation. Instead of a single monolithic feed-forward network within each transformer block, MoE introduces multiple specialized "expert" subnetworks. A gating mechanism dynamically selects a subset of these experts to activate for each token. In practice, this means only a fraction of the total parameters are engaged during any given inference step. For example, a model might contain eight expert networks per layer but activate only two per token. The total parameter count may appear massive on paper, yet the active parameter count—the portion actually used per token—remains significantly smaller.

This sparse activation strategy redefines efficiency. It allows models to scale total capacity without proportionally scaling inference cost. Performance approaches that of larger dense models, but with compute closer to much smaller systems. Mixtral's implementation proved that open-weight models could leverage sparse architectures while maintaining strong reasoning and language benchmarks. The innovation lies not in inventing MoE as a concept—it has academic roots—but in deploying it effectively within an open-weight, production-grade LLM.

For sovereign intelligence, this architectural shift is profound. Efficiency is not only about memory compression or quantization; it is also about structural economy. MoE architectures offer a path toward scaling capability while preserving manageability. When fewer parameters are active per token, latency decreases and hardware requirements become more flexible. Organizations that cannot afford hyperscale clusters benefit disproportionately from these gains.

The strategic importance of Mistral's contribution also lies in diversification of innovation geography. Europe's regulatory climate emphasizes data protection, transparency, and digital sovereignty. An advanced open-weight model emerging from that environment reinforces the idea that high-performance AI need not be monopolized by a small global subset of actors. It strengthens the narrative that distributed research communities can compete through architectural ingenuity rather than brute-force compute budgets alone.

Mixtral also sparked broader discussion about modularity. If expert subnetworks can specialize implicitly during training, then future models might explicitly encode domain specialization within architecture. Instead of fine-tuning entire monolithic models, different experts could align to different domains, activated contextually by the gating network. This introduces the possibility of scalable specialization within a single unified model framework.

In practical terms, the Mixture of Experts approach shifts how developers interpret parameter counts. A 40+ billion parameter MoE model does not necessarily require the same inference cost profile as a 40B dense model. Capacity becomes decoupled from activation. This reframing encourages experimentation beyond simple scaling.

Mistral's open-weight release amplified this architectural idea across the global open-source community. Developers could inspect, benchmark, quantize, and deploy these models locally. The result was not just a competitive European model, but a redistribution of design thinking. Efficiency became structural rather than purely hardware-dependent. In doing so, Mixtral expanded the toolkit for sovereign AI, proving that architectural elegance can substitute for raw scale and that openness can coexist with cutting-edge performance.

Llama 3 represents a maturation point in the evolution of open-weight large language models. Earlier releases in the LLaMA family proved that high-quality foundational models could be shared beyond the walls of hyperscale providers, but Llama 3 refined that vision with stronger alignment, improved reasoning, better multilingual performance, and more deliberate ecosystem integration. It signaled that open-weight models were no longer experimental alternatives to closed systems—they were competitive engines capable of powering serious applications.

The evolution from earlier releases is visible in both scale and refinement. The first generation of LLaMA models demonstrated that relatively efficient architectures trained on curated datasets could rival larger dense systems. Llama 2 expanded licensing clarity and pushed usability for commercial environments. Llama 3 advanced further in training data diversity, alignment robustness, and benchmark performance. Improvements in instruction-following and longer context handling made it more adaptable for enterprise workflows. The training corpus expanded in scale and quality, reducing common failure modes such as hallucination drift and shallow reasoning patterns.

One of the defining impacts of Llama 3 was its effect on community confidence. When a model with competitive benchmarks is released with open weights, it fundamentally alters development incentives. Researchers can replicate evaluations, fine-tune models for domain tasks, and experiment with optimization strategies without building from scratch. Startups can integrate powerful base models locally rather than tying their product entirely to API contracts. The psychological shift matters: open-weight performance parity dismantles the assumption that cutting-edge capability must remain closed.

Performance benchmarks reinforced this transition. Llama 3 achieved strong results across reasoning tasks, coding benchmarks, math evaluations, and general language understanding tests. While benchmark numbers never capture full real-world behavior, they provide standardized indicators of progress. The gap between open-weight and proprietary systems narrowed significantly. Competitive scores on datasets like MMLU, HumanEval, and reasoning challenges gave enterprises empirical reassurance that open deployment did not require sacrificing quality.

Ecosystem support amplified the model's reach. Tools such as Ollama simplified local deployment for developers by packaging models into easily runnable containers with minimal configuration. vLLM improved inference throughput through optimized memory management and parallelization strategies, enabling high-performance server deployments for production workloads. Additional frameworks integrated quantization pipelines, LoRA fine-tuning workflows, and vector database connectors. The surrounding tooling transformed Llama 3 from a downloadable artifact into a practical building block within sovereign AI stacks.

Quantization compatibility further democratized usage. With 4-bit and 8-bit variants available, even large parameter versions of Llama 3 could operate on high-memory consumer GPUs. This compressed deployment capacity extended sophisticated inference beyond enterprise clusters into home labs, research institutions, and startups with constrained budgets. Combined with LoRA-based customization, Llama 3 became a flexible substrate rather than a rigid monolith.

Best use cases for Llama 3 align with its balance of performance and deployability. It excels in knowledge-intensive text generation, coding assistance, summarization pipelines, and conversational agents embedded within enterprise systems. Because weights are inspectable and fine-tunable, it adapts effectively to regulated industries requiring localized compliance control. Educational tools, internal copilots, document analysis systems, and domain-specific assistants benefit from its instruction alignment and scalable architecture. In hybrid architectures, Llama 3 often serves as the primary local reasoning engine, augmented by retrieval pipelines to ground responses in proprietary data.

Its release also reinforced a broader strategic principle: open-weight models thrive when ecosystems mature around them. Performance alone does not create adoption. Tooling, deployment frameworks, quantization support, benchmarking transparency, and community iteration create compounding effects. Llama 3 became not merely a model but a platform anchor within a growing open ecosystem.

The deeper significance lies in trajectory. Each iteration tightened the feedback loop between open research and applied deployment. Community fine-tunes proliferated rapidly, spawning domain-adapted variants and optimized inference builds within weeks. Sovereign intelligence became less about proving viability and more about refining specialization.

Llama 3 stands as evidence that open-weight AI can sustain momentum across multiple generations, integrating architectural improvement with community distribution. It underscores a transition from experimental openness to operational reliability, strengthening the case that advanced language modeling does not need to remain locked behind centralized endpoints.

GPT-OSS represents the conceptual bridge between frontier-scale research and distributed sovereignty. It embodies the idea that high-capability generative models can be released with open weights while still preserving responsible alignment frameworks and enterprise-grade usability. The notion challenges the long-held assumption that advanced language intelligence must remain exclusively cloud-hosted and API-gated. Instead, GPT-OSS suggests a model family engineered from inception with open-weight deployment as a first-class objective rather than an afterthought.

The concept of open-weight releases in this context goes beyond symbolic transparency. It means the trained parameters—the core statistical representation of the model's learned knowledge—are distributed in a form that allows local inference, adaptation, and integration. Open-weight does not necessarily imply fully open training data or unrestricted replication of the original training pipeline. It signifies that the inferential engine itself can operate under user control. This structural shift changes both technical incentives and governance dynamics. Developers can audit behaviors directly. Enterprises can stress-test edge cases without submitting proprietary data to external endpoints. Researchers can build derivative systems atop a shared foundation.

However, releasing powerful weights raises alignment considerations. GPT-OSS-type initiatives emphasize that openness must coexist with guardrails. Alignment frameworks become modular components layered into the deployment stack rather than hardcoded black boxes exclusively controlled by a vendor. Instruction tuning datasets, reinforcement learning pipelines, safety classifiers, and policy constraints are provided alongside the model. Organizations may choose to adopt default alignment profiles or adjust them according to regulatory and operational needs. The emphasis shifts from centralized enforcement to configurable safety architectures.

This modular alignment model allows enterprises to balance control and responsibility. For example, a healthcare system deploying GPT-OSS internally might integrate domain-specific safety filters ensuring outputs comply with medical standards and privacy regulations. A financial institution could embed compliance auditing layers that log reasoning chains for regulatory review. Rather than a single global policy dictating acceptable outputs, alignment becomes an adaptable layer reflecting contextual governance requirements. Open-weight architecture enables safety not only through restriction but through inspectable constraint design.

Intended deployment models for GPT-OSS prioritize flexibility. The architecture supports standalone inference nodes for home lab enthusiasts, clustered GPU environments for enterprise-scale throughput, and hybrid stacks that combine local reasoning with retrieval or cloud augmentation. Quantization support ensures operability across hardware tiers. Containerized deployment templates streamline integration into Kubernetes clusters or private cloud environments. The guiding principle is portability: the model should function wherever compute exists, not solely within a specific provider's infrastructure.

In many envisioned deployments, GPT-OSS operates as the cognitive core inside broader AI orchestration systems. Retrieval-augmented pipelines connect it to vector databases containing proprietary documents. API layers expose endpoints internally without routing external traffic.

Authentication gateways ensure user segmentation and access control. Observability tooling tracks inference latency and behavioral anomalies. The goal is to transform an open-weight model into a production-ready reasoning engine embedded within enterprise architectures rather than treated as an experimental artifact.

Enterprise use scenarios illustrate the practical implications of such a release. Corporations can deploy GPT-OSS as an internal copilot integrated into email systems, documentation workflows, code repositories, and analytics dashboards. Sensitive contracts or intellectual property never leave the organization's perimeter. Legal departments can train domain-specific adapters for regulatory language. Engineering teams can optimize inference throughput for CI/CD pipelines generating documentation and test cases automatically. Multinational organizations can deploy region-specific instances aligned with local data residency laws.

Cost structure also plays a role in enterprise adoption. With open weights, the financial model shifts from per-token operational expenditure toward infrastructure investment and amortized compute costs. Organizations running high-volume workloads benefit from reduced marginal inference expenses once hardware is deployed. Predictable budgeting replaces variable token pricing. The transparency of deployment enables capacity planning that aligns with enterprise IT strategies.

Another strategic dimension involves resilience and continuity. Enterprises deploying GPT-OSS locally are less vulnerable to sudden API deprecations or service interruptions. Model versions can be frozen for consistency, tested before upgrades, and migrated on controlled schedules.

This capability appeals to regulated sectors where stability and auditability are paramount.

Beyond individual companies, GPT-OSS-like initiatives have broader ecosystem implications. They encourage third-party optimization, independent benchmarking, and derivative innovations. Communities may develop enhanced quantization pipelines, domain adapters, or inference engines tailored for specialized accelerators. This collaborative amplification accelerates model capability beyond what a single organization could accomplish alone.

The philosophical implication is equally significant. GPT-OSS reframes advanced language modeling as shared infrastructure rather than proprietary oracle. It suggests a future in which cutting-edge models can coexist with decentralized governance frameworks, configurable alignment layers, and distributed deployment models. Enterprise AI strategy shifts from "Which endpoint do we subscribe to?" toward "Which version do we operate, tune, and govern ourselves?"

In this framework, open weights become the keystone of sovereign intelligence. Alignment frameworks provide structured responsibility. Deployment flexibility ensures operational integration. Enterprise scenarios demonstrate real-world viability. GPT-OSS becomes less a single product name and more a blueprint: a model family architected for openness, aligned safety, and scalable autonomy, bridging the gap between frontier research and locally controlled cognitive infrastructure.

Falcon emerged as one of the most consequential open-weight releases outside the traditional Silicon Valley ecosystem, demonstrating that large-scale foundation model development could be executed by research institutions operating beyond the dominant U.S.–China axis. Built by the Technology Innovation Institute in the United Arab Emirates, Falcon signaled that sovereign AI ambitions were not theoretical. They were executable with sufficient coordination, funding, and infrastructure. Its release contributed to the narrative that advanced language modeling could become geographically diversified rather than consolidated in a few hyperscale labs.

The training scale behind Falcon was central to its credibility. Unlike smaller open projects trained on limited curated datasets, Falcon was developed using extensive corpora and substantial compute resources. Its training data reportedly included refined web text sourced from large-scale filtered crawls, carefully deduplicated and quality-controlled to maximize signal-to-noise ratio. Data preprocessing emphasized linguistic breadth and structural diversity, combining natural language prose with code and structured text patterns. This large and refined dataset allowed Falcon to compete not merely as an academic exercise but as a serious general-purpose model.

Compute investment played an equally defining role. Training Falcon required thousands of high-performance GPUs running in distributed parallel configurations over extended periods. This level of compute was critical for achieving meaningful scaling. Empirical scaling laws suggest that performance improves predictably with increases in parameters, training tokens, and total compute. Falcon leveraged this principle by combining substantial dataset exposure with a parameter count designed to balance capability and practicality. The result was a model that performed competitively across multiple standardized benchmarks relative to similarly sized systems.

Performance relative to parameter efficiency became a defining narrative around Falcon. At equivalent parameter counts, Falcon achieved strong results on reasoning, comprehension, and coding evaluations. In certain benchmarks, it outperformed models with higher nominal parameter counts. This outcome highlighted that parameter size alone is not the sole determinant of quality. Dataset composition, training stability, architectural tuning, and optimization methods can significantly influence outcomes. Falcon's dense architecture demonstrated that thoughtful data engineering and clean training pipelines could yield performance density—more capability per parameter.

Parameter efficiency matters because it shapes deployability. A model with 40 billion parameters that approaches or exceeds the performance of a denser 65 billion parameter alternative offers economic advantages. It requires less VRAM for inference and can be quantized more easily for local deployment. This reduction in resource requirements expands access across research institutions and enterprises operating without hyperscale budgets. Falcon helped reinforce the idea that efficiency in training translates directly into sovereignty in deployment.

Falcon also influenced discussion around open licensing frameworks. Its release was accompanied by licensing conditions that enabled research and many forms of commercial use but included structured restrictions designed to prevent misuse or certain large-scale exploitative deployments without agreement. This licensing approach reflects the broader tension in open-weight AI between permissive freedom and responsible governance. Fully permissive licenses maximize adoption but offer little control over downstream use. More structured licenses attempt to balance openness with ethical guardrails and strategic control.

Commercial licensing clarity is critical for enterprise adoption. Organizations evaluating Falcon must understand whether integration into revenue-generating products is permitted, whether derivatives must preserve attribution, and whether specific industries are excluded. Falcon's licensing signaled seriousness about enabling business integration while retaining some policy oversight. This hybrid model acknowledges commercial reality while avoiding a purely unrestricted release that could undermine developer responsibility or institutional interests.

Beyond performance metrics, Falcon's symbolic significance cannot be overstated. It demonstrated that training at meaningful scale was not reserved for established U.S.-based AI leaders. It contributed to a multipolar AI development landscape. In doing so, it strengthened the case for sovereign model initiatives globally. Countries and organizations seeking strategic autonomy in AI could look to Falcon as proof of concept: high-quality open-weight systems could be built with targeted investment and technical coordination.

Falcon's legacy extends into the ecosystem it catalyzed. After release, the open-source community rapidly experimented with quantization techniques, fine-tuning adapters, and optimized inference pipelines. Integration into frameworks such as local inference engines and distributed serving stacks accelerated adoption. Each community optimization amplified the model's practical value beyond its original training envelope.

Performance versus parameter efficiency remains an enduring theme in model evaluation. Falcon showed that careful training strategies can produce systems that punch above their numerical scale. It reinforced that engineering quality often matters as much as raw size. In a world where compute cost remains a barrier, this insight shapes strategic decisions about where to invest.

Falcon stands as both a technical and geopolitical milestone. It combines substantial training scale with efficient performance characteristics and structured commercial licensing. Together, these attributes positioned it as a serious participant in the open-weight movement and strengthened the global argument that advanced AI can be developed, governed, and deployed beyond centralized corporate silos.

Phi represents a deliberate inversion of the prevailing assumption that bigger is always better in language modeling. At a time when the dominant narrative in AI development emphasized exponential scaling—more parameters, more tokens, more compute—Phi demonstrated that carefully designed small models could achieve surprising levels of capability through disciplined data curation and curriculum-based training. Rather than chasing raw parameter growth, Phi emphasized efficiency, instructional clarity, and learning quality. Its significance lies not in rivaling the absolute performance of frontier-scale systems, but in proving that capability density—intelligence per parameter—can be strategically optimized.

Small model efficiency begins with architectural discipline. When parameter counts remain in the low billions rather than tens or hundreds of billions, every weight must justify its existence. The training data cannot be indiscriminately scraped and filtered only lightly; it must be selected and structured. Phi's approach focused on curated datasets emphasizing high-signal examples over sheer volume. The training process privileged educational structure, reasoning clarity, and logically coherent problem-solving material rather than the broad but noisy sprawl of general web text. By compressing signal into fewer parameters, the model effectively learned more from less.

Curriculum-based training became a cornerstone of this philosophy. Rather than exposing the model to all difficulty levels randomly, training data was sequenced or weighted to simulate progressive learning stages. Easier foundational reasoning tasks established representational scaffolding. More complex, multi-step problems were introduced later. This design mirrors human pedagogy, where understanding builds incrementally. In practice, curriculum structuring stabilizes training and encourages deeper pattern internalization. Instead of memorizing superficial correlations across vast noisy corpora, the model develops structured reasoning heuristics grounded in high-quality examples.

This focus on curated learning also addresses data efficiency. Large foundation models often rely on trillion-token corpora because quantity compensates for noise. Phi demonstrated that disciplined selection and structured exposure can reduce the need for astronomical scale. While it cannot escape scaling laws entirely—performance still correlates with compute and parameters—it optimizes within constrained budgets. This reorientation matters for sovereign AI ecosystems where compute access may be limited.

Edge-device optimization is where Phi's design philosophy becomes particularly impactful. Models in the 1–5 billion parameter range can operate on consumer-grade GPUs and, with aggressive quantization, even on powerful CPUs or mobile-class accelerators. This accessibility expands deployment possibilities beyond server rooms and data centers. Educational applications can embed reasoning engines inside offline tablets. Robotics systems can integrate local language understanding without persistent cloud connectivity. Enterprises can distribute inference nodes across secure networks where transmitting data externally is prohibited.

Smaller models also offer advantages in latency and energy consumption. Because inference scales roughly linearly with parameter count in dense architectures, reducing size directly reduces computational overhead per token. Lower memory footprints decrease VRAM pressure, enabling deployment on hardware configurations that would be impractical for large models. For real-time interactive systems—voice assistants, embedded control interfaces, augmented reality overlays—this latency efficiency becomes decisive. Sovereign intelligence at the edge is not merely about privacy; it is about responsiveness.

There are also strategic resilience advantages. Smaller models are easier to replicate, version, and distribute. They can be fine-tuned more rapidly for specialized domains using

LoRA or QLoRA techniques. Organizations experimenting with domain adaptation benefit from shorter training cycles and reduced infrastructure cost. This accelerates iteration. Instead of committing vast compute to fine-tune massive systems, teams can prototype adaptations quickly and deploy them widely.

The principle of "when smaller beats bigger" emerges in several specific contexts. For narrowly defined tasks—structured data extraction, deterministic formatting, educational tutoring at controlled difficulty levels—a small, well-aligned model can outperform a larger, more diffuse system. Larger models may overgeneralize, hallucinate creatively, or introduce unnecessary complexity. Smaller models, when trained on high-signal curriculum data, often produce more predictable outputs. In compliance-focused industries, predictability can outweigh raw generative sophistication.

Cost dynamics reinforce this advantage. Infrastructure investment scales dramatically with parameter size. A model that achieves acceptable reasoning accuracy at one-tenth the parameter count may require a fraction of the hardware expenditure. For startups and educational institutions, this makes advanced AI deployment financially viable. Even for large enterprises, smaller models can serve as dedicated subsystems within broader AI architectures, handling routine tasks while reserving heavyweight models for complex queries.

Phi also reframes competitive benchmarking. Instead of asking whether a small model matches the absolute frontier, the relevant question becomes efficiency-adjusted performance. How much reasoning quality is delivered per gigabyte of VRAM? How much inference throughput per watt of power? These metrics matter in decentralized and mobile environments. As AI integrates into physical devices—from industrial controllers to personal electronics—the balance shifts toward lean architectures optimized for environment-specific constraints.

The broader philosophical implication is that intelligence scaling is multidimensional. Parameter count is one axis, but data quality, curriculum sequencing, architecture tuning, and hardware-aware optimization form additional axes. Phi's existence challenges the inevitability of monolithic scale dominance. It demonstrates that thoughtfully engineered compact systems can achieve meaningful autonomy.

In sovereign AI contexts, small efficient models serve as building blocks. They can operate independently in offline settings, populate distributed nodes across secure infrastructures, or function as specialized task processors within orchestrated systems. When combined with retrieval mechanisms or modular adapters, their effective knowledge range expands without inflating parameter size.

Phi stands as evidence that intelligent capability is not exclusively proportional to mass. Through curriculum-based learning, disciplined data curation, and hardware-conscious optimization, smaller models can punch far above their numerical weight. In doing so, they broaden the path toward accessible, deployable, and resilient AI systems that do not require hyperscale backing to function effectively.

Qwen represents one of the most important developments in the global evolution of open-weight language models, particularly in demonstrating that large-scale AI capability is not geographically monocentric. Developed within China's advanced AI research ecosystem, Qwen reflects a deliberate strategy to scale multilingual intelligence while maintaining competitive reasoning and coding performance. Its emergence reinforces the idea that sovereign AI efforts are unfolding simultaneously across multiple regions, each optimizing models according to linguistic, economic, and regulatory priorities.

Multilingual scaling is central to Qwen's identity. Many early large language models were disproportionately optimized for English due to dataset availability and benchmarking conventions. Qwen expanded training emphasis across Mandarin Chinese and additional languages, enabling stronger bidirectional translation, comprehension, and reasoning in multilingual contexts. Multilingual scaling is not trivial; tokenization, vocabulary selection, and dataset balancing significantly influence performance parity. When training data volume favors one language, models often exhibit fluency imbalances. Qwen's development strategy emphasized more equitable token representation and high-quality regional corpora, improving its ability to operate fluidly across linguistic boundaries.

Scaling across languages also enhances cross-cultural reasoning. Idiomatic expressions, region-specific terminology, and policy nuances require contextual sensitivity. By embedding diverse linguistic structures into training, Qwen strengthens its adaptability across local knowledge domains.

This multilingual competence positions it as particularly valuable in environments where cross-border commerce, diplomacy, and multicultural user bases intersect. The model's ability to integrate Chinese-language knowledge resources alongside English and other languages broadens its applicability beyond monolingual benchmarks.

Instruction-tuned variants play a crucial role in Qwen's ecosystem. Like many modern LLM families, Qwen includes base pretrained versions alongside instruction-aligned releases. The instruction-tuned variants refine task adherence, dialogue consistency, and safe response behavior. This layered architecture allows developers to choose between raw foundational capacity and conversationally optimized versions depending on deployment needs. In enterprise contexts, instruction tuning ensures more predictable interactions and structured output formatting, critical for workflow automation.

These instruction variants often extend into specialized domains such as coding, mathematical reasoning, and business analysis. Targeted fine-tuning on domain-relevant datasets increases performance without necessitating entirely new architectures. This modular release philosophy mirrors broader open-weight movements: distribute a capable base model, then provide aligned and task-focused derivatives to accelerate integration.

Enterprise usage in Asia highlights Qwen's strategic positioning. Large organizations operating within China and across East Asia face regulatory frameworks emphasizing data localization and sovereign control. Deploying cloud-based foreign AI services may be impractical or restricted under certain compliance regimes. Qwen offers an alternative grounded within the regional ecosystem, compatible with domestic infrastructure and aligned with local regulatory expectations. Enterprises can host instances within private data centers, ensuring sensitive financial, governmental, or industrial data does not traverse external jurisdictions.

Industries such as manufacturing, logistics, telecommunications, and fintech benefit from such deployments. Qwen's multilingual competency supports cross-border operations linking East Asian markets with global partners. It can serve as a translation intermediary, a documentation assistant, or a data interpretation engine within multilingual supply chains. Moreover, instruction-aligned versions can integrate directly into internal knowledge management systems, customer service automation pipelines, and compliance auditing workflows.

Cross-regional deployment underscores Qwen's broader strategic relevance. As international enterprises operate across continents, the need for models capable of functioning within distinct regulatory and linguistic environments becomes paramount. Open-weight or semi-open-weight distributions allow multinational firms to deploy region-specific instances while retaining architectural consistency. A company could operate a Qwen-based model in Asia for Mandarin-heavy workloads while synchronizing structured interfaces with deployments elsewhere.

Interoperability becomes critical in such architectures. Integration layers connecting retrieval systems, translation modules, and compliance filters must function across jurisdictions. Qwen's multilingual foundation supports such integration by reducing fragmentation between regional deployments. Instead of relying on separate monolingual systems for each language cluster, organizations can standardize around a unified multilingual backbone.

From a competitive standpoint, Qwen reinforces multipolar AI evolution. It narrows perceived performance gaps between Western-developed open-weight models and Asian counterparts. Benchmarks demonstrate its competence in reasoning, math, and coding tasks relative to similarly scaled models globally. This competitive parity ensures that innovation remains geographically distributed rather than concentrated.

Strategically, Qwen exemplifies how sovereign AI initiatives combine technical scale with policy alignment. Multilingual design increases global utility. Instruction variants facilitate enterprise integration. Regional hosting strengthens regulatory compliance. Cross-regional adaptability supports multinational deployment. Together, these features position Qwen as more than a regional model; it becomes a critical node within the distributed architecture of global open-weight intelligence.

In the broader narrative of sovereign AI, Qwen demonstrates that openness and performance need not be constrained by geography. Advanced language models can arise in diverse ecosystems, tuned for linguistic richness and regulatory alignment. As AI infrastructure continues decentralizing, multilingual scaling and cross-regional flexibility will become not optional features but foundational requirements.

DeepSeek represents one of the most strategically interesting developments in the modern open-weight ecosystem because it centers explicitly on reasoning capability rather than raw conversational fluency. While many language models emphasize breadth—general knowledge, stylistic versatility, or broad instruction-following—DeepSeek's trajectory has focused on structured problem-solving, mathematics, coding logic, and multi-step reasoning tasks. This specialization reframes what competitiveness means in the open-weight landscape. Instead of simply matching surface-level benchmark scores, DeepSeek aims to close the reasoning gap that often separates open models from frontier proprietary systems.

Reasoning-focused models require deliberate training design. They depend heavily on datasets containing step-by-step solutions, formal logic exercises, code execution traces, mathematical proofs, and structured analytical writing. The objective is not merely to predict fluent next tokens but to internalize solution pathways. This approach influences how training corpora are assembled and filtered. High-quality reasoning examples—especially those that explicitly articulate intermediate steps—shape gradient updates in ways that improve logical consistency across token sequences.

One of the most important phenomena associated with reasoning-focused models is the emergence of chain-of-thought behaviors. Chain-of-thought refers to the model's ability to articulate intermediate reasoning steps before arriving at a final answer. Early research showed that prompting large models to "think step by step" improved performance on math and logic tasks. DeepSeek's training design appears to internalize that pattern more directly, making structured reasoning less dependent on prompt engineering tricks. The model does not merely output final answers; it generates coherent internal sequences of logical transformations.

Chain-of-thought emergence is not magic; it is a function of representation learning at scale combined with exposure to structured reasoning examples. When a model sees enough examples that demonstrate incremental solution building, the statistical patterns of reasoning become embedded in its parameter space. What distinguishes DeepSeek is the explicit emphasis on this capability as a primary design objective rather than an incidental byproduct of general-scale training.

Competing with frontier models in reasoning domains is particularly difficult. Proprietary systems benefit from immense compute budgets, massive training datasets, and reinforcement tuning cycles that optimize not just correctness but structured clarity. For an open-weight model to approach that level of reasoning fidelity, it must optimize efficiently. DeepSeek's performance on coding benchmarks, mathematical reasoning tasks, and analytical challenges signaled that open-weight systems could narrow the cognitive performance gap. This matters for sovereign AI initiatives because reasoning competence underpins high-value enterprise applications—legal analysis, quantitative modeling, scientific research assistance, and software engineering workflows.

Another important dimension of DeepSeek's development is the provision of lightweight alternatives. Not every deployment requires maximal reasoning scale. Smaller DeepSeek variants enable users with more constrained hardware to access capable reasoning engines. Through architecture tuning, quantization compatibility, and parameter-efficient adaptation, these lighter versions preserve strong logical capabilities while reducing deployment requirements. This balance extends the sovereign deployment argument: advanced reasoning need not remain confined to hyperscale environments.

The release of DeepSeek V3 marked a particularly strategic moment. V3 was notable not only for its performance benchmarks but for its training efficiency relative to capability. Lowering training costs directly strengthens the sovereignty narrative. Training frontier-scale models traditionally demands extraordinary compute expenditure, concentrating capability among organizations with deep capital reserves. If a model family demonstrates that competitive reasoning can be achieved with significantly reduced compute budgets, the barrier to entry shifts.

Lower training cost does not merely reduce research expense; it decentralizes innovation. Smaller research labs, national institutions, and specialized enterprises gain the theoretical capacity to replicate or build upon similar architectures. Efficiency compacts the compute-to-capability ratio. If V3 achieves near-frontier reasoning performance without near-frontier compute investment, it validates the argument that scale need not be synonymous with exclusivity.

Cost efficiency at training time also affects inference economics indirectly. More efficient training pipelines often correlate with architectural optimizations that streamline inference pathways. Sparse activation, improved parameter initialization strategies, and refined optimization schedules can reduce redundant computation. When combined with quantization and hardware-aware fine-tuning, these efficiencies cascade into practical deployment advantages.

DeepSeek's evolution underscores a broader principle: the race is not purely about being the largest; it is about extracting maximum reasoning density from available compute. For sovereign AI ecosystems, reasoning density translates into autonomy density. Organizations that can host high-competency reasoning systems locally gain independence in core analytic tasks. They no longer require continuous API dependency to perform structured decision-support operations.

The psychological impact of DeepSeek's reasoning benchmarks is also significant. It signals that open ecosystems are capable of tackling the hardest cognitive domains. Math and code reasoning have often served as proxy indicators for deeper structural capability. By demonstrating strength in these areas, DeepSeek contributes to the perception shift that open-weight models can be serious analytical instruments rather than lightweight conversational tools.

In the larger arc of sovereign intelligence, DeepSeek functions as both technical proof and strategic symbol. It shows that chain-of-thought behaviors can be systematically cultivated, that reasoning performance can approach frontier models without identical budgets, and that training efficiency advances reshape the economics of AI development. With V3 reducing training cost barriers, the sovereign argument strengthens: advanced cognitive infrastructure can be built, improved, and deployed without exclusive dependence on hyperscale incumbents.

Local deployment is where the philosophy of sovereign intelligence becomes operational reality. Running a model locally means inference occurs on hardware you control, within networks you manage, under policies you define. Prompts, embeddings, logs, and outputs remain inside your perimeter. Latency becomes predictable. Versioning becomes deliberate. The stack becomes inspectable end-to-end: model weights, quantization format, runtime engine, retrieval layer, and orchestration logic. This shift transforms AI from a remote service into embedded infrastructure.

Ollama has become one of the simplest entry points into local LLM deployment. It abstracts away much of the configuration complexity by packaging models into self-contained runtimes that can be pulled and executed with minimal setup. Under the hood, it manages model downloads, caching, quantized variants, and hardware detection. Users can run instruction-tuned models locally with a single command, expose REST endpoints for application integration, and swap models quickly for benchmarking or experimentation. Ollama's value lies in its accessibility: it lowers the friction between downloading open weights and running a responsive local assistant.

LM Studio targets a slightly different audience. It provides a graphical interface for downloading, configuring, and running local models without requiring extensive command-line fluency. It integrates GGUF-compatible models, supports quantized builds, and provides conversational testing environments. For developers, researchers, and enterprise teams exploring sovereign deployment options, LM Studio serves as a rapid prototyping interface. It helps validate hardware compatibility, measure VRAM utilization, and compare decoding strategies before production integration.

Dockerized inference extends local deployment from hobbyist experimentation to production architecture. Containerization allows AI runtimes to operate in isolated, reproducible environments. A Docker image can encapsulate the inference engine, model weights, Python dependencies, CUDA libraries, and configuration files. When deployed, the container behaves identically across machines, minimizing environment drift. In enterprise settings, containers integrate seamlessly with orchestration platforms such as Kubernetes, enabling horizontal scaling, load balancing, and failover strategies. Dockerized inference decouples model lifecycle management from host operating systems, enabling smoother updates and rollback control.

GPU server builds represent the next tier of sovereign infrastructure. For serious deployments handling sustained workloads, a dedicated inference server becomes necessary. Hardware selection begins with GPUs optimized for tensor workloads. High-memory cards—such as RTX 3090s, 4090s, or professional-grade accelerators—determine the maximum parameter size and quantization precision possible. VRAM capacity is critical; models must fit within memory constraints alongside runtime overhead. Multi-GPU configurations allow model sharding or parallel request handling, increasing throughput.

Power supply and thermal management become engineering considerations. GPUs operating at sustained load generate significant heat and draw high wattage. Proper airflow, liquid cooling options, and reliable PSU ratings prevent thermal throttling and instability. Fast NVMe storage ensures rapid model loading and retrieval operations. Ample system RAM supports vector databases and concurrent processes. Linux-based operating systems typically offer the most stable CUDA and driver compatibility, though Windows-based inference remains viable for certain configurations.

Network configuration also matters. A local GPU server deployed within a private LAN can expose internal APIs secured by authentication layers. Reverse proxies and SSL termination ensure encrypted communication. Logging and monitoring tools track GPU utilization, latency, and memory consumption. For organizations, this transforms the AI server into a first-class infrastructure node comparable to application or database servers.

The build philosophy balances performance, cost, and scalability. Quantized 4-bit or 8-bit models reduce VRAM demands, allowing high-capability systems to operate on consumer-grade GPUs. Larger dense models may require multiple GPUs connected via NVLink or PCIe optimization to enable memory pooling. Inference engines such as vLLM or llama.cpp can be tuned for throughput versus latency tradeoffs, depending on workload type.

Local deployment is not merely about hardware acquisition; it is about architectural ownership. When a team can download open weights, quantize them, package them in containers, and deploy them onto GPU servers they built or provisioned, sovereignty moves from theory to implementation. Ollama simplifies access. LM Studio accelerates experimentation. Docker enables reproducible production. GPU server builds provide computational foundation.

Together, these elements form a layered stack: model weights at the base, runtime engine above, containerization for portability, hardware infrastructure for scale, and application interfaces at the top. Each layer remains within the operator's control. In this structure, intelligence becomes a managed internal service rather than a metered external endpoint. Local deployment is where independence stops being philosophical and becomes technical.

Building an AI workstation is the physical manifestation of sovereign intelligence. It transforms abstract model weights into executable capability living on hardware you own and control. The configuration of that hardware determines what size models you can run, how fast they respond, how efficiently you can fine-tune them, and how resilient your system remains under load. Unlike general-purpose desktops, AI workstations are built around compute density, memory bandwidth, and thermal stability.

At the center of any AI workstation is the GPU. For inference workloads, VRAM capacity is more important than raw gaming performance. A budget tier build typically includes a single high-memory consumer GPU such as an RTX 3060 12GB, RTX 4070 Ti, or RTX 3090 24GB. This tier is ideal for running quantized 7B–13B parameter models comfortably, experimenting with 30B-class models at 4-bit precision, and performing light LoRA fine-tuning. It represents the accessible entry point for individual developers and researchers exploring sovereign deployments.

The mid-tier setup usually features a 24GB or higher GPU, often the RTX 3090 or 4090 class, paired with a modern multi-core CPU and at least 64GB of system RAM. This configuration can handle larger quantized 70B models using memory-efficient formats or multi-GPU bridging in some cases. It supports more aggressive experimentation, including parameter-efficient fine-tuning and running retrieval-augmented pipelines simultaneously with inference. For startups or advanced hobbyists, this tier provides a strong balance between capability and cost.

Professional-tier workstations move into multi-GPU territory. Dual 3090s, dual 4090s, or data-center-grade GPUs such as A100 or H100 accelerators drastically expand inference and training potential. Multi-GPU configurations enable model parallelism for large dense models or improve throughput by serving concurrent requests. These setups require enterprise-grade motherboards with sufficient PCIe lanes, high-wattage power supplies, and advanced cooling configurations. Professional builds are appropriate for organizations serving internal AI applications at scale or conducting sustained research.

CPU selection plays a secondary but important role. While GPUs handle tensor computation, CPUs coordinate orchestration, retrieval indexing, containerization, and background services. Multi-core processors from recent Intel or AMD generations provide ample headroom for inference servers and vector database operations. Excessively expensive CPUs rarely improve raw inference performance unless heavy data preprocessing or simultaneous workloads are involved.

System RAM must complement VRAM. Large embeddings databases, document corpora, and concurrent pipelines consume significant memory outside the GPU. For budget builds, 32GB may suffice, though 64GB provides better stability. Professional setups often use 128GB or more, especially when running multiple containers or complex orchestration layers.

Storage strategy is frequently underestimated. Large models occupy tens or hundreds of gigabytes depending on parameter count and quantization format. Fine-tuned variants multiply that footprint. Fast NVMe SSDs are essential for rapid model loading and retrieval performance. A common strategy involves a primary NVMe drive dedicated to operating system and active models, with secondary high-capacity SSDs for archival storage of checkpoints and datasets.

For sustained experimentation, separating data and model storage from the OS improves maintainability. A tiered storage design might include a smaller high-speed NVMe drive for inference hot-load models and a larger but slightly slower SSD array for long-term storage. This segmentation reduces bottlenecks and simplifies backup routines.

RAID configurations become relevant in professional environments. RAID 0 offers performance benefits by striping data across drives but provides no redundancy. RAID 1 mirrors data for safety at the cost of halved effective capacity. RAID 5 and RAID 10 balance performance and redundancy but require multiple drives and careful configuration. For AI workstations storing irreplaceable training data or fine-tuning checkpoints, redundancy is critical. A mirrored storage volume ensures that hardware failure does not result in catastrophic data loss.

Redundancy extends beyond storage. High-quality power supplies with sufficient headroom prevent instability under GPU load spikes. Surge protection and uninterruptible power supplies safeguard against sudden outages during fine-tuning sessions. Effective thermal design—large case airflow, liquid cooling loops, or rack-mounted chassis with optimized ventilation—ensures hardware longevity under sustained tensor operations.

Budget and professional setups reflect different strategic priorities. A budget workstation focuses on accessibility, enabling local deployment and experimentation without excessive capital expense. It empowers individual sovereignty. A professional workstation prioritizes throughput, redundancy, and scalability, embedding AI capability into organizational infrastructure. Both serve the broader sovereign philosophy but operate at different performance envelopes.

Ultimately, building an AI workstation is not merely assembling parts; it is defining your capability ceiling. GPU choice determines model size. VRAM determines precision and parallelism. Storage determines experimentation agility. Redundancy determines reliability. Each decision shapes how independent your AI stack becomes. When the workstation powers up and loads a model without reaching outward to a remote endpoint, sovereignty shifts from theory to silicon.

Security and isolation sit at the core of true sovereign AI deployment. Running a model locally is only the first step; ensuring that the surrounding environment protects sensitive data and model integrity completes the sovereignty loop. When large language models are embedded into internal workflows—processing proprietary documents, legal contracts, financial projections, research datasets, or classified materials—the security architecture must be as deliberate as the compute architecture. Sovereign intelligence without isolation remains vulnerable.

Air-gapped deployments represent the most extreme form of isolation. In an air-gapped configuration, the AI workstation or inference server is physically and logically disconnected from external networks. There is no outbound internet access, no cloud synchronization, and no remote update channel. Model weights are transferred via controlled physical media, and software updates are vetted before installation. This configuration is common in defense, critical infrastructure, and sensitive research environments. By eliminating network pathways, the attack surface shrinks dramatically. Remote exploitation, data exfiltration, and unauthorized telemetry become structurally impossible.

Air-gapping changes operational discipline. Because systems cannot automatically pull updates or dependencies, organizations must maintain curated internal repositories for drivers, inference engines, and security patches. Model upgrades are intentionally staged and validated in controlled environments before production deployment. This slower cadence reinforces stability. The model becomes an internal asset governed by local change control procedures, not an externally evolving service.

Encryption underpins another critical layer of sovereignty. Even in isolated networks, physical hardware theft or internal compromise remains possible. Encrypted volumes protect stored model weights, embeddings databases, and fine-tuning datasets at rest. Full-disk encryption ensures that if a workstation is removed from its environment, the stored information remains inaccessible without authentication keys. Key management becomes central—passphrases, hardware security modules, or TPM-based mechanisms must be implemented responsibly to avoid introducing new vulnerabilities.

For AI workflows, encrypted volumes serve dual purposes: protecting proprietary datasets used for fine-tuning and safeguarding customized adapters that encode domain-specific knowledge. Fine-tuned models often encapsulate valuable intellectual property. A LoRA adapter trained on internal codebases, legal precedents, or industrial process documentation effectively becomes a condensed representation of institutional knowledge. Protecting these artifacts is as important as protecting source documents themselves.

Private fine-tuning pipelines extend the security perimeter into the training process. Fine-tuning involves exposing the base model to curated datasets and updating adapter weights accordingly. If this pipeline routes data through external compute or shared infrastructure, the sovereignty guarantee weakens. A private pipeline ensures that both data preprocessing and gradient computation occur within trusted environments. Dedicated GPU servers process datasets locally, and intermediate checkpoints remain within encrypted storage volumes.

Isolation during fine-tuning also reduces the risk of data leakage through logging systems or telemetry. Organizations should audit logging configurations to ensure that input prompts, training examples, and error traces are not exported beyond secure boundaries. Containerized environments add a further isolation layer, preventing interference between fine-tuning jobs and other services running on shared hardware. Role-based access controls restrict which personnel can initiate training runs or access generated adapters.

Security posture must also include network segmentation for non–air-gapped environments. Internal inference servers should reside in private subnets accessible only through authenticated gateways. API endpoints exposed within enterprise networks should require encryption protocols such as TLS and robust token authentication. Monitoring systems should track unusual query patterns, which could indicate misuse or prompt injection attempts aimed at extracting sensitive information.

Hardware-level security complements these software measures. BIOS locks, secure boot configurations, and firmware validation reduce the risk of tampering. Trusted Platform Modules can help manage encryption keys and attest to system integrity during startup. In high-security deployments, rack-mounted servers reside in controlled data rooms with restricted physical access.

The cultural dimension of security matters as well. Sovereign AI implies not only technical control but operational discipline. Teams must adopt clear protocols for dataset ingestion, model version control, and permission management. Change logs document modifications to weights or alignment layers. Backup policies ensure that encrypted archives exist in physically separate locations.

Isolation is not an obstacle to innovation; it is a foundation for trust. When organizations know their models operate inside controlled boundaries, they are more willing to integrate AI deeply into core workflows. Legal teams gain confidence. Compliance officers gain auditability. Researchers gain freedom to explore sensitive problem spaces without external data risk.

In sovereign architectures, security is inseparable from ownership. Air-gapped deployments provide maximum isolation. Encrypted volumes protect intellectual assets at rest. Private fine-tuning pipelines maintain confidentiality during adaptation. Together, these elements transform a local model from a technical convenience into a secure cognitive infrastructure node—controlled, auditable, and defensible.

Prompt engineering was the first phase of mainstream interaction with large language models. Users discovered that phrasing mattered. Asking a model to "act as a lawyer," "think step by step," or "respond in JSON format" could radically change output quality. Entire disciplines emerged around crafting better prompts—adding constraints, examples, tone cues, role descriptions, and structured instructions. While this unlocked impressive results, it also revealed a limitation: prompt engineering treats the model as a single-turn oracle. The interaction remains bound to the chat box. The user supplies text, the model returns text, and nothing persists beyond the exchange unless external systems manage it.

As organizations began integrating AI into real workflows, the fragility of prompt-only systems became apparent. A single well-crafted prompt may perform adequately in isolation, but enterprise tasks require memory, tool usage, error handling, data retrieval, and state management. A real workflow does not end when text is generated; it begins. Reports need to be saved to disk. APIs need to be called. Databases must be queried. Emails must be drafted and scheduled. In these scenarios, the model's output is only one step within a broader operational chain.

Moving beyond the chat box means embedding models into systematic workflows. Rather than relying on a human repeatedly pasting instructions, organizations design structured pipelines where the model receives controlled inputs, performs transformations, invokes tools, and passes outputs to subsequent processes. This reframes the model from conversational partner to cognitive component. Prompt engineering remains important, but it becomes embedded within larger orchestration systems that provide repeatability and reliability.

Agentic frameworks emerged to support this transition. Tools such as LangChain, AutoGPT, and CrewAI extend open models beyond text generation. They enable models to interact with external systems, execute code, browse web content, manipulate files, and coordinate multi-step tasks autonomously. The key architectural shift is granting the model controlled access to tools and memory layers. Instead of returning a final answer immediately, the model can reason about which action to take next.

In an agentic architecture, the model operates within a loop. It receives a goal, evaluates available tools, selects an action, executes that action, observes the result, and iterates. This allows the system to gather additional information before responding, correct mistakes dynamically, or chain multiple operations together. For example, an agent might search the web for current data, summarize key findings, write the summary into a structured report, and save it to a designated file location—all without human intervention between steps.

LangChain provides a modular framework for constructing such pipelines. It connects large language models to vector databases, APIs, file systems, and other software components. Developers define chains of actions and memory buffers that allow state persistence across interactions. The model's reasoning becomes part of a deterministic execution environment, reducing randomness and increasing control.

AutoGPT popularized the concept of autonomous goal-driven agents. Instead of supplying detailed instructions each time, a user defines a high-level objective. The system iteratively decomposes that objective into sub-tasks, executes them through tool calls, and refines its approach based on intermediate outcomes. While early implementations revealed reliability challenges, the architectural concept was transformative: models could initiate actions rather than only respond.

CrewAI expands this idea by introducing multi-agent orchestration. Rather than one monolithic model handling every task, specialized agents collaborate. One agent may conduct research, another may critique results, and another may synthesize outputs into final deliverables. This division of labor mirrors organizational structures in human teams. It also allows for clearer role definition, modular tuning, and improved scalability.

Agentic workflows amplify the value of open-weight models in sovereign environments. When models run locally, and tools are integrated within private networks, the entire workflow remains under organizational control. An agent can browse internal documentation repositories rather than the public web. It can update internal databases securely. It can operate within permission scopes defined by enterprise security policies.

Moving beyond prompt engineering also introduces stronger reproducibility. Structured workflows can be version-controlled. Tool configurations can be audited. Action logs can be preserved. Unlike ephemeral chat interactions, systematic agents produce traceable execution trails. This is essential in regulated industries where decisions must be explainable and auditable.

The distinction between prompt engineering and systematic workflows parallels the difference between scripting and software engineering. Prompt engineering is exploratory and adaptive, effective for human-guided tasks. Agentic systems formalize those interactions into programmable infrastructures. They transform AI from a conversational novelty into a functional subsystem capable of performing concrete operations.

In sovereign AI deployments, this transition is critical. A locally hosted model gains far greater utility when integrated into structured workflows. Writing files, executing controlled browsing, manipulating structured data, and interacting with APIs convert generative capacity into operational capacity. Intelligence moves from the interface into the infrastructure. The model is no longer confined to producing text inside a chat window; it becomes an actor within a controlled computational ecosystem, capable of doing rather than merely responding.

Model commoditization is the phase where large language models stop being mystical breakthroughs and start becoming interchangeable infrastructure components. In the earliest waves of generative AI, a small number of frontier labs produced systems that seemed categorically superior to anything available elsewhere. Access to these systems carried prestige, competitive leverage, and strategic dependency. Over time, however, the gap between elite frontier models and high-quality community models began to narrow. When multiple open-weight releases achieve strong benchmark parity across reasoning, coding, and language understanding tasks, the model itself shifts from rare asset to commodity substrate.

The distinction between frontier and community models historically centered on scale and secrecy. Frontier models were trained with immense compute budgets, proprietary datasets, and closed evaluation pipelines. Their weights were restricted.

Their architecture details often remained opaque. Community models, by contrast, prioritized openness and iteration. They emerged from universities, decentralized research labs, startups, or collaborative ecosystems. Initially, these models lagged behind in raw capability. Over time, the innovation loop tightened. Community researchers learned from published scaling methods, optimization techniques, and dataset curation strategies. Quantization, LoRA fine-tuning, sparse architectures, and improved tokenization pipelines collectively reduced performance gaps.

As community models approached functional parity for many real-world tasks, differentiation shifted. Enterprises no longer selected models purely on benchmark deltas; they evaluated integration ease, cost predictability, alignment flexibility, and sovereignty considerations. A 3% benchmark advantage became less decisive if a community model could be hosted locally with near-zero marginal cost per query. The calculus favored deployability and control over absolute maximum performance in niche metrics.

The parameter arms race illustrates another dimension of commoditization. Early competitive signaling emphasized parameter counts. Larger numbers implied greater intelligence. Companies escalated into tens of billions, then hundreds of billions, then trillions of parameters. However, scaling laws revealed diminishing returns beyond certain thresholds if data quality and architecture improvements did not keep pace. At the same time, infrastructure costs increased dramatically. The arms race began to encounter physical and economic constraints—memory ceilings, energy budgets, cooling requirements.

As more organizations reached large parameter territory, sheer scale stopped being a unique differentiator. A 70B model from one lab could perform similarly to a 65B model from another if both were well-trained and instruction-aligned. Community releases eroded the exclusivity of large parameter counts. The arms race shifted toward quality-of-training, structured reasoning, and efficiency per parameter rather than raw expansion alone.

Efficiency breakthroughs disrupted the arms race further. Quantization reduced deployment requirements. Mixture-of-experts architectures allowed sparse activation of large total parameter counts. Improved optimizers and curriculum-based training reduced required training tokens. Retrieval-augmented generation externalized knowledge storage, reducing the pressure to encode all facts in parameters. Parameter-efficient fine-tuning allowed domain adaptation without retraining entire models. Each efficiency gain weakened the monopoly power of sheer computational scale.

Commoditization also changes pricing structures. When multiple capable open-weight models become available, the value proposition shifts upward in the stack. Instead of competing solely on model intelligence, providers compete on orchestration layers, safety tooling, retrieval integration, enterprise support, and ecosystem compatibility. The foundational model becomes infrastructure akin to a database engine. Competitive advantage lies in how well that infrastructure is wrapped, secured, and integrated rather than in its mere existence.

In sovereign intelligence frameworks, commoditization is empowering. If high-quality models are available openly and regularly updated, organizations can treat models as replaceable components. Upgrading versions becomes a managed operation rather than a vendor-dependent negotiation. Fine-tuning adapters can be migrated across compatible architectures. Deployment strategies emphasize modularity.

This transition mirrors previous technological cycles. Databases, operating systems, and web servers once differentiated companies at the infrastructure level. Over time, open standards and broad competition reduced those tools to baseline components. Innovation shifted toward applications built atop them. AI models are undergoing a similar shift. The intellectual gravity moves from "Who owns the smartest model?" to "Who builds the most effective systems on top of widely available intelligence?"

Efficiency breakthroughs accelerate this process by democratizing competence. When a mid-sized research team can train competitive models without hyperscale budgets, new entrants multiply. When quantized variants allow advanced reasoning on consumer hardware, dependence erodes. When sparse architectures provide frontier-like capability with constrained active compute, economic barriers shrink.

Model commoditization does not eliminate frontier research. Advanced labs will continue exploring larger context windows, multimodal fusion, and reasoning depth. But commoditization ensures that baseline capability becomes broadly accessible. It reshapes competition from exclusivity toward integration, governance, and application design.

The long-term effect is structural normalization. Intelligence engines become like compilers or relational databases—essential, powerful, but no longer singularly dominant. Sovereign intelligence thrives under commoditization because choice increases, dependency decreases, and infrastructure ownership becomes realistic. In this environment, the model is no longer the moat; it is the foundation.

The regulatory landscape surrounding artificial intelligence is evolving as rapidly as the technology itself. Governments worldwide are attempting to balance innovation with safety, economic competitiveness with national security, and openness with accountability. AI is no longer viewed solely as a research domain or commercial product; it is increasingly classified as critical infrastructure with implications for defense, finance, healthcare, labor markets, and information integrity. As a result, regulatory frameworks are emerging that reshape how models are trained, distributed, and deployed.

Global AI regulation trends reveal divergence rather than uniformity. The European Union has advanced comprehensive, risk-based legislation aimed at categorizing AI systems according to potential harm. High-risk systems face strict transparency, documentation, and auditing requirements. The emphasis is on accountability, explainability, and human oversight. Meanwhile, the United States has pursued a more decentralized approach, relying on executive orders, agency-level guidance, and sector-specific oversight. Rather than a single sweeping framework, U.S. regulation often focuses on procurement standards, national security safeguards, and voluntary commitments. Asian regulatory environments vary widely, with some countries emphasizing industrial acceleration and digital sovereignty while others adopt strict content and data governance requirements.

These differing approaches create a fragmented global landscape. Enterprises operating across borders must navigate inconsistent definitions of high-risk AI, varying documentation demands, and divergent data residency rules. Multinational organizations increasingly design AI infrastructure with regulatory adaptability in mind, deploying localized instances to comply with regional standards. Sovereign AI strategies often emerge in response to this fragmentation, allowing organizations to host and manage models within jurisdictions aligned to their legal obligations.

Export controls add another layer of complexity. Governments have placed restrictions on the export of advanced semiconductor hardware, high-performance GPUs, and certain AI training technologies. These controls aim to protect national security interests and maintain technological advantage. Limiting access to cutting-edge accelerators constrains who can train frontier-scale models and shifts competitive dynamics. Export controls do not only affect model developers; they cascade down to hardware procurement strategies for research labs and enterprises.

In addition to hardware restrictions, regulatory bodies have begun scrutinizing the dissemination of advanced AI model weights. Concerns about misuse, dual-use capabilities, and the rapid proliferation of powerful reasoning systems have sparked debate over whether certain high-capability models should face export classification similar to sensitive technologies. This introduces tension between open-weight distribution and national security policy. If a model exceeds defined capability thresholds, questions arise about whether unrestricted global release is permissible.

The open-source movement occupies a complex position in this environment. On one hand, openness aligns with transparency goals. Inspectable models allow researchers to audit bias, test safety claims, and build safeguards collaboratively. Open-source development enables decentralized safety experimentation rather than concentrating governance authority within a few corporate entities. From a regulatory standpoint, transparency can support trust.

On the other hand, regulators worry about uncontrolled proliferation. Unlike cloud-based APIs where providers can enforce usage policies, open-weight releases can be downloaded and modified without centralized oversight. Once weights circulate, enforcement becomes difficult. Policymakers grapple with the idea that open distribution might facilitate misuse, including malicious automation, disinformation campaigns, or unauthorized weaponization. This creates tension between values of openness and concerns about governance control.

Some proposals aim to reconcile this tension through tiered release frameworks. Models below certain capability thresholds remain widely accessible, while higher-tier systems might require registration, licensing, or conditional access agreements. Others advocate for voluntary safety commitments tied to open-weight releases, including model cards, usage guidelines, and pre-release red-teaming reports.

These approaches attempt to balance decentralization with accountability without undermining the collaborative benefits of open research.

Data governance forms another regulatory axis. Laws concerning data privacy, copyright, and personal data rights influence how models are trained and fine-tuned. Questions surrounding the legality of large-scale web scraping, the use of copyrighted materials in training corpora, and the treatment of personal information have led to lawsuits and policy debates. Organizations developing sovereign AI stacks must evaluate not only deployment security but also dataset provenance and licensing compliance.

Environmental regulation is emerging as a subtle but influential factor. Training large models consumes significant energy. Governments increasingly evaluate the carbon footprint of data centers and may impose sustainability standards. Efficient architectures and quantization techniques become not only economic advantages but regulatory alignments.

The future regulatory environment is likely to remain dynamic. Policymakers strive to encourage innovation while mitigating systemic risks. Industry groups lobby for flexible frameworks that avoid stifling research. Civil society advocates demand stronger transparency and human rights safeguards. Within this evolving negotiation, sovereign AI strategies provide structural resilience. Hosting and governing models locally allows organizations to adapt to regulatory shifts without depending entirely on external providers.

Regulation does not inherently conflict with sovereignty. In many cases, sovereignty strengthens compliance by enabling direct oversight, audit logging, and localized control. The tension arises when governance aims to centralize authority over technology that inherently benefits from distributed collaboration. The challenge for the coming decade will be aligning openness with responsibility in ways that preserve innovation while addressing legitimate security and ethical concerns.

Personal AI sovereignty begins with a simple shift in mindset: intelligence is not something you rent, it is something you host. For most users today, AI exists as a service endpoint—an assistant accessed through a browser tab, bound to someone else's infrastructure, memory policies, and update schedule. Personal sovereignty reimagines that relationship. Your AI "brain" lives on hardware you control. It runs within your network. It remembers on your terms. It evolves with your data, not as a side effect of a platform's global training cycle.

Running your own AI brain means deploying a model locally and embedding it into your digital life in a persistent, structured way. This goes beyond installing an application. It involves integrating inference servers with local storage, embedding pipelines, encrypted archives, and indexing systems. The model becomes a cognitive layer over your personal information ecosystem. It summarizes your documents, drafts emails in your voice, recalls past decisions, and surfaces patterns across years of accumulated data. Because it runs locally, the prompts and outputs never traverse external servers unless you explicitly allow them to.

Owning your knowledge graph is the next evolution of this idea. A knowledge graph is not merely a folder structure or search index; it is a semantic map connecting your documents, conversations, notes, projects, and ideas. Each file becomes more than static text—it becomes a node in a network of relationships. Emails link to meeting notes. Research PDFs connect to annotated highlights. Journal entries connect to goals and timelines. When this graph is indexed locally using embeddings and vector search, your AI model can retrieve relevant connections in context, not just keyword matches.

This ownership transforms search into reasoning. Instead of typing a term into a generic search bar, you ask questions about your own history. "When did I first discuss this project?" "What decisions did I make about that investment?" "Summarize the evolution of my thinking on this topic." The model retrieves relevant nodes from your indexed graph and synthesizes responses grounded in your own data. The intelligence is not simply generative; it is reflective.

Avoiding platform lock-in is a core motivation behind personal sovereignty. When personal data accumulates inside proprietary ecosystems, switching costs become psychological and technical barriers. Your email archives, writing drafts, project notes, and digital conversations become entangled with interfaces you do not control. Cloud assistants may process that data, but they do not grant exportable, inspectable control over the indexing logic or embedding models applied to it. A sovereign AI architecture decouples cognition from platform dependence. Data resides in open formats. Models operate locally. Vector databases can be migrated. You retain the freedom to upgrade, replace, or fine-tune the model without relinquishing your data history.

Digital continuity extends this concept across time. Platforms rise and fall. APIs deprecate. Companies pivot or collapse. But your knowledge accumulates across decades. A locally maintained AI brain ensures that your accumulated digital memory remains accessible independent of corporate survival timelines. Version upgrades occur on your schedule. Archival backups ensure persistence. Even if external services disappear, your indexed graph remains intact.

Local retrieval-augmented generation becomes the practical engine of personal memory. In this architecture, documents are chunked into manageable segments and converted into vector embeddings using a local embedding model. These vectors populate a private database optimized for similarity search. When you ask a question, the system retrieves semantically relevant segments from this database and injects them into the context window of your local LLM. The model then generates a response grounded explicitly in your own material.

This design avoids the need to encode your entire history into model parameters. Instead, knowledge remains external but indexed. The LLM becomes a reasoning interface rather than a static repository. As your archive grows, you simply add more embeddings. There is no need to retrain the base model. The memory layer expands modularly.

The dream of sovereign AI is not merely a smarter chatbot. It is a cognitive partner that has indexed every email, PDF, annotation, and note you have ever created—securely, privately, and locally. It recalls context you have forgotten. It reconstructs threads of thought across years. It drafts with stylistic continuity because it has absorbed your prior language patterns through local retrieval. It suggests connections because it can see semantic similarities across domains you might not consciously connect.

Privacy underpins this dream. If your entire digital archive feeds into a remote API, true ownership vanishes. Local RAG ensures that sensitive communications, financial documents, private reflections, and creative drafts never leave your perimeter. Encryption safeguards storage. Access controls restrict who can query the memory layer. The result is an AI that knows you deeply without exposing you externally.

Personal sovereignty also changes creative workflows. Writers can query their own archives for conceptual continuity. Researchers can trace hypothesis evolution across notebooks. Entrepreneurs can analyze patterns in historical deal correspondence. Instead of manually browsing folders, the AI reconstructs narratives and surfaces insights.

There is also a psychological dimension. Knowing that your AI brain operates independently of external corporate interests fosters autonomy. Updates do not arbitrarily shift tone or introduce hidden alignment changes without your consent. You choose which model version governs your memory. You decide when to integrate new capabilities.

Personal AI sovereignty reframes intelligence from rented assistance to sustained partnership. It integrates memory, reasoning, and continuity into a locally governed architecture. By running your own model, owning your knowledge graph, resisting lock-in, and implementing local retrieval as personal memory, you create an enduring digital extension of yourself—private, persistent, and under your control.

A glossary of terms in artificial intelligence is not merely a list of definitions; it is an orientation map. The vocabulary of large language models and open-weight systems can seem opaque at first glance, yet each term describes a specific mechanical reality inside the machine. Understanding these terms dissolves the mystique and replaces it with structure. What follows is an expanded conceptual grounding of some of the most foundational ideas: tokens, parameters, inference, and quantization.

Tokens are the fundamental units of language that a model processes. When you type a sentence into a language model, it does not see words in the way humans do. Instead, the text is broken into smaller segments called tokens. A token might be a whole word, part of a word, punctuation, or even a space depending on the tokenization system used. For example, the word "running" might be split into "run" and "ning" or represented as a single token depending on how frequently it appears in training data. Tokenization exists because neural networks operate numerically, not linguistically. Each token is mapped to a numerical ID and represented as a vector embedding before entering the transformer network.

Token count matters for multiple reasons. During training, models process massive numbers of tokens—often in the trillions—to learn statistical relationships between them. During inference, token count directly influences cost and performance. Every prompt consumes input tokens, and every generated word consumes output tokens. Context windows also operate in tokens, meaning a model may only "remember" a fixed number of tokens at a time before older ones fall outside its active attention span. Tokens are therefore the currency of interaction, learning, and memory.

Parameters are the adjustable numerical weights inside a neural network. They are not stored knowledge in a literal sense but represent learned correlations between patterns in data. When a model is described as having 7 billion parameters or 70 billion parameters, it refers to the number of these numerical weights. Each parameter is typically a floating-point number that influences how strongly one neuron connects to another. During training, parameters are adjusted through gradient descent to minimize prediction error. Over time, these adjustments encode patterns of grammar, reasoning structures, factual associations, and stylistic tendencies.

More parameters generally allow a model to represent more complex relationships, but parameter count alone does not guarantee quality. Data quality, training duration, architecture design, and alignment processes all affect outcome. Parameters also influence deployment feasibility. Larger parameter counts require more memory and compute. Smaller, well-trained models may outperform larger but poorly trained ones in certain domains. In sovereign AI strategies, parameter efficiency—intelligence per parameter—becomes more important than raw size.

Inference is the process of using a trained model to generate predictions or outputs. Unlike training, inference does not modify parameters. It is the forward pass of information through the network using already learned weights. When you submit a prompt, the model converts tokens into embeddings, processes them through transformer layers, calculates probability distributions over possible next tokens, and then selects one according to the decoding strategy. That prediction becomes the next token, and the process repeats iteratively until a stopping condition is met.

Inference speed depends on hardware, model size, and optimization techniques. GPUs accelerate matrix multiplications required by transformer layers. Decoding strategies influence determinism and variability. Greedy decoding selects the most probable next token, producing deterministic output. Sampling methods introduce randomness to improve creativity or diversity. Inference is computationally expensive at scale but far less resource-intensive than training, which requires gradient computation and parameter updates.

Quantization is the process of reducing the numerical precision of model parameters to decrease memory footprint and computational load. Standard training often uses 16-bit floating-point numbers or higher precision formats. These representations offer accuracy but require significant memory. Quantization converts these weights into lower precision formats such as 8-bit or 4-bit integers. This compression dramatically reduces VRAM requirements while preserving most of the model's functional behavior.

Quantization makes local deployment feasible. Without it, large models would require enterprise-grade accelerators with vast memory capacity. A 70-billion-parameter model stored at 16-bit precision may require roughly 140GB of VRAM, placing it beyond reach for most individuals. With 4-bit quantization, that requirement can shrink to a fraction of its original size, enabling deployment across consumer GPUs. Advanced quantization techniques preserve performance by selectively retaining higher precision in sensitive layers while compressing others more aggressively.

These four terms—tokens, parameters, inference, and quantization—form the structural backbone of modern large language models. Tokens define the units of interaction. Parameters encode learned statistical structures. Inference performs real-time reasoning using those structures. Quantization enables practical deployment by optimizing memory and compute usage. Together, they represent the mechanics underlying what appears externally as fluid conversational intelligence.

Understanding this vocabulary transforms AI from abstraction into engineering. It clarifies the difference between scale and efficiency, between training and deployment, between stored weights and retrieved knowledge. As sovereign AI ecosystems expand, literacy in these terms becomes not optional but essential. They describe the levers through which individuals and organizations shape, host, and govern their own intelligence systems.

Hardware benchmark tables are essential for translating abstract model sizes into practical deployment decisions. They answer a fundamental sovereign AI question: what hardware do I actually need to run this model effectively? Below are structured benchmark reference tables focused on inference workloads for open-weight large language models. These assume modern transformer architectures and common quantization formats (16-bit, 8-bit, 4-bit). Actual performance varies based on inference engine, cooling, driver versions, and workload configuration, but these provide realistic working ranges.

GPU VRAM Requirements by Model Size (Inference Only)

Model Size FP16 (16-bit) VRAM 8-bit VRAM 4-bit VRAM

7B ~14–16 GB ~8–10 GB ~4–6 GB

13B ~26–28 GB ~14–16 GB ~7–9 GB

30B ~60 GB ~30–34 GB ~16–20 GB

65B/70B ~130–140 GB ~70–80 GB ~35–45 GB

Mixture-of-Experts (e.g., 8x7B active 2) behaves closer to a 12–15B dense model per token during inference.

These numbers reflect raw model weight storage. Add 10–20% VRAM overhead for runtime, KV cache, and inference engine requirements.

Consumer GPU Benchmark Table (Inference Tokens/sec, Approximate)

GPU Model VRAM 7B 4-bit 13B 4-bit 70B 4-bit (sharded) RTX 3060 12GB 12 GB 30–40 t/s 15–22 t/s Not feasible RTX 3090 24 GB 60–80 t/s 35–50 t/s Dual GPU required RTX 4090 24 GB 75–100 t/s 45–65 t/s Dual GPU required Dual 3090 48 GB — — 18–28 t/s Dual 4090 48 GB — — 22–35 t/s

Tokens per second vary depending on context size, temperature, and KV cache length.

Professional / Datacenter GPU Benchmarks

GPU Model VRAM 70B 4-bit 70B 8-bit Notes A100 40GB 40 GB ~25–35 t/s Not single-GPU Capable of single 70B 4-bit A100 80GB 80 GB ~45–65 t/s ~30–45 t/s Handles 70B 8-bit single GPU H100 80GB 80 GB ~60–90 t/s

~40–60 t/s Significantly better bandwidth L40S 48 GB ~25–40 t/s Moderate Strong price/perf ratio

CPU-Only Inference (Quantized)

CPU Model 7B 4-bit 13B 4-bit Ryzen 9 / i9 high core 5–10 t/s 2–5 t/s Server-grade EPYC/Xeon 10–15 t/s 5–8 t/s

CPU inference is feasible for experimentation but unsuitable for high-throughput production without acceleration.

Recommended Hardware Tiers

Entry-Level Sovereign Setup GPU: RTX 3060 12GB or RTX 4070 Use Case: 7B–13B quantized models, local RAG, experimentation Cost Efficiency: High Limitation: Cannot run large 30B+ models comfortably

Power User / Developer Setup GPU: RTX 3090 or RTX 4090 (24GB) RAM: 64GB+ Use Case: 13B–30B models, LoRA fine-tuning, serious local workflows Strong sweet spot for sovereign AI enthusiasts

Advanced Sovereign Enterprise Node GPU: Dual 4090 or Dual 3090 (48GB total) RAM: 128GB+ Use Case: 70B 4-bit inference, internal copilot systems Capable of handling moderate concurrent users

Professional Production Server GPU: A100/H100 class RAM: 256GB+ Use Case: High-volume internal enterprise inference High capex, lower marginal cost per query at scale

Storage Benchmark Guidance

Model weights: 7B quantized: 4–8 GB 13B quantized: 8–16 GB 70B 4-bit: 35–45 GB

Embedding database: 1 million document chunks ≈ 2–8 GB depending on vector size.

Fast NVMe SSD is strongly recommended. HDD is not suitable for active model hosting.

Throughput Scaling Notes

Throughput improves with: • Faster memory bandwidth (GDDR6X vs older generations) • Multi-GPU model sharding • Optimized inference engines (vLLM, TensorRT-LLM, llama.cpp with CUDA) • Batch processing (useful for servers, not chat latency)

Latency tends to increase with: • Larger context windows • Higher precision (8-bit vs 4-bit) • Long output generations

Cost Efficiency Estimate (Consumer Hardware)

Scenario: Dual RTX 4090 system (~$3,500–$5,000 build cost) Amortized over 3 years: Monthly hardware cost ≈ $100–$150 Marginal inference cost ≈ near-zero (electricity only) Compared to API token billing at scale, break-even occurs surprisingly fast for heavy usage environments.

Interpretation for Sovereign AI Strategy

These tables demonstrate a critical point: hardware capability defines your sovereignty ceiling. A single high-end consumer GPU today can comfortably run models that rival frontier systems from only a few years ago. Dual GPU systems can host 70B-class models locally with quantization. Datacenter accelerators unlock enterprise-scale concurrency.

Quantization and memory optimization are what bridge the gap between hyperscale and personal deployment. Without 4-bit inference, large models would remain effectively inaccessible. With it, sovereign intelligence becomes a matter of engineering choice, not corporate permission.

Hardware benchmarking is therefore not just performance trivia—it is strategic infrastructure planning.

Licensing determines what you are actually allowed to do with a model after you download it. Performance benchmarks tell you how well a system thinks. A license tells you whether you can deploy it in production, fine-tune it, redistribute it, sell access to it, or modify it freely. In sovereign AI strategy, licensing clarity is as important as parameter count. Below is a structured comparison matrix of common license types seen in AI model releases, followed by interpretation guidance for enterprise and independent developers.

License Type Comparison Matrix

License Type Commercial Use Modify / Fine-Tune Redistribute Copyleft (Share-Alike) Competitive Restrictions Typical Examples

MIT / BSD Yes Yes Yes No No Many open-source codebases

Apache 2.0 Yes Yes Yes No No Open model tooling, frameworks

GPL / AGPL Yes Yes Yes Yes No Some inference engines

Open-RAIL (various) Yes (conditional) Yes (conditional) Yes (conditional) No Often usage restrictions Some image/text models

Custom Open-Weight Sometimes Yes Limited No Often yes (scale/competitor) Several modern LLM families

Research-Only No Yes (research only) No commercial No N/A Academic releases

Proprietary API No (self-host) No No N/A Vendor controlled Cloud-only models

Permissive Open-Source Licenses (MIT, BSD, Apache 2.0)

Permissive licenses are the most flexible. They allow commercial use, modification, private deployment, redistribution, and integration into proprietary systems with minimal obligations. Apache 2.0 includes explicit patent protection, which is why many enterprises prefer it over pure MIT. These licenses are highly aligned with sovereign deployment because they do not restrict local hosting, competitive usage, or derivative commercialization. If a model or tool is released under MIT or Apache 2.0, it is generally safe for startups and enterprises to build revenue-generating products around it.

Copyleft Licenses (GPL, AGPL)

Copyleft licenses require that derivative works also remain open under the same license. GPL applies primarily to distributed software; AGPL extends this obligation to network usage, meaning if you modify and deploy the system as a service, you may be required to release your modifications publicly. These licenses promote community reciprocity but may discourage commercial adoption in proprietary environments. From a sovereignty perspective, they guarantee ongoing openness but may restrict closed enterprise customization strategies.

Open-RAIL and Responsible AI Licenses

Open-RAIL-style licenses emerged specifically in AI contexts. They allow access to model weights and often permit commercial use but impose behavioral restrictions. For example, certain misuse categories (surveillance abuse, biometric targeting, unlawful generation tasks) may be explicitly prohibited. These licenses attempt to reconcile openness with ethical governance. However, enforcement mechanisms are often unclear, and organizations must interpret compliance risk carefully.

Custom Open-Weight Licenses

Several modern large model families use custom licenses. These often permit research and many forms of commercial use but restrict certain competitive scenarios, such as using the weights to train a competing foundation model above a specific parameter threshold. Some also require explicit agreements for extremely large-scale deployment. These licenses are designed to allow ecosystem development while preserving economic positioning for the original publisher. From an enterprise standpoint, careful legal review is required before deploying at scale.

Research-Only Licenses

Research-only licenses permit download and experimentation but prohibit commercial deployment. These are common in academic releases or early-stage models. They are suitable for universities and evaluation but unusable for revenue-generating applications. Sovereign deployment is technically possible under such licenses but legally constrained to non-commercial contexts.

Proprietary API Access

Although not technically a "license" in the traditional open-source sense, cloud-hosted proprietary APIs operate under terms of service rather than redistribution licenses. You cannot download weights, fine-tune independently, or self-host. Commercial use is typically allowed under subscription agreements, but all deployment remains vendor-controlled. From a sovereignty standpoint, API access represents maximum dependency and minimum architectural autonomy.

Key Licensing Considerations for Sovereign AI

Commercial Rights

Can you sell a product built on the model? If not explicitly allowed, you are exposed to legal risk.

Fine-Tuning Rights

Some licenses allow inference but restrict training derivatives beyond certain thresholds.

Redistribution

If you fine-tune a model, can you redistribute the modified version? Permissive licenses say yes; others impose limits.

Competitive Clauses

Some modern LLM licenses restrict usage if your product directly competes with the licensor's hosted service. This can affect startup positioning.

Scale-Based Triggers

Certain licenses impose additional obligations once usage exceeds defined thresholds (e.g., user count, revenue, or parameter size in derivative training).

Strategic Licensing Implications

For personal sovereign AI deployments, permissive or open-weight licenses typically suffice since you are not redistributing commercially. For startups building AI-native applications, license clarity becomes mission-critical. A license that appears open but includes scale-based competitive clauses can become restrictive as your product grows.

Enterprises should treat licensing as infrastructure risk assessment. Model replacement capability is important. Avoiding license lock-in is similar to avoiding vendor lock-in.

Maintaining deployment modularity across compatible architectures allows flexibility if licensing terms change in future versions.

Sovereignty and License Philosophy

There is a spectrum between full permissive open-source and full proprietary API control. The sovereign AI thesis depends not just on technical feasibility but legal permissibility. True sovereignty requires the ability to download, modify, host, adapt, and scale without asking permission.

Licensing clarity ensures that the intelligence stack you build today remains viable tomorrow. A powerful model without deployment rights is not sovereign. A permissively licensed model you can host, fine-tune, and redistribute within your organization becomes infrastructure under your governance.

In the long arc of AI commoditization, licensing frameworks will shape which models become foundational public utilities and which remain constrained ecosystems. Understanding the matrix is therefore not optional—it is strategic literacy for building durable AI systems.

Here's a clean, step-by-step "first local deployment" path that gets you from zero → running a local model → optionally adding local RAG. I'm assuming a typical Windows/Mac/Linux laptop or desktop. No headings, no bullets, just the sequence.

Step 1: Confirm what you're deploying on. If you have an NVIDIA GPU, install the latest NVIDIA driver first. If you're on Mac (Apple Silicon), you can still run local models but performance depends on unified memory. If you're CPU-only, you can still run smaller quantized models, just slower. You don't need perfect hardware to start; you just need a working baseline.

Step 2: Pick the easiest runtime so you actually succeed on day one. For most people, that's Ollama or LM Studio. Ollama is fastest if you're comfortable with a terminal. LM Studio is fastest if you want a GUI and zero command-line.

Step 3: Install Ollama (fastest "it just works" path). Download and install it for your OS. Once installed, open a terminal and confirm it runs by checking that the service starts. Then pull a small, reliable model first so you don't hit hardware limits immediately. A great first choice is a 7B–8B instruction model in 4-bit. Run it, ask a few questions, and confirm it responds smoothly. If it's slow, that's okay; it means you're likely CPU-only or running out of VRAM, and you should use smaller models.

Step 4: Verify that your model is truly local. Turn off Wi-Fi or disconnect ethernet and run the same prompt again. If it still answers, you've confirmed local inference. This is the moment where "sovereignty" becomes real.

Step 5: Move from "chat" to "API" so you can integrate it into workflows. Ollama can expose a local endpoint so your other tools can call it. Test the endpoint with a simple request from your browser or a local REST client. Once you can get a response from an API call, you've graduated from "local chat" to "local infrastructure."

Step 6: Pick a model upgrade path based on your hardware ceiling. If you have 8–12GB VRAM, stay in the 7B–13B class at 4-bit. If you have 24GB VRAM, you can run 30B-class models at 4-bit and some 70B variants only if you shard across multiple GPUs. Don't chase giant models immediately; get reliability first.

Step 7: Add a basic folder-based "personal memory" using local RAG. Choose a small set of documents—ten PDFs, a handful of notes—so you can validate the pipeline quickly. The key is not indexing everything at once. Split documents into chunks, embed them into vectors, and store them in a local vector database. Then implement retrieval: for any question, retrieve the top relevant chunks and prepend them into the prompt. When the model answers with citations from your files, you've built your first private memory layer.

Step 8: Make your RAG trustworthy. Add three simple rules: always return the quoted source chunk when making factual claims, refuse to guess when retrieval returns nothing relevant, and show the filenames and chunk IDs used. This immediately reduces hallucinations and makes the system usable for real work.

Step 9: Harden the setup so it survives daily use. Put your models on fast storage (NVMe if possible). Back up your vector database and your document folder. If you change models, keep the old one around until you confirm behavior stability. If your goal is long-term continuity, stability matters more than novelty.

Step 10: Upgrade from "single-user workstation" to "local server" when you're ready. If you want multiple devices in your house or office to use your local model, you can run the inference runtime on one machine and expose it over your LAN behind authentication. That turns one workstation into an internal AI service.

Step 11: Add private fine-tuning only after you've used RAG for a while. Many people jump straight to fine-tuning when RAG will solve 80% of the "my model doesn't know my stuff" problem. Fine-tuning is best for behavior, style, formatting, and specialized reasoning patterns—not for stuffing facts. Start with LoRA on small datasets. Keep it reversible.

Step 12: Create your first "real workflow" so you stop living in the chat box. Choose something concrete like: "Summarize these three PDFs into a 1-page brief and save it as a markdown file." If your local system can read files, retrieve relevant chunks, generate a structured output, and save it locally, you've reached the point where open-weight models become truly useful.

Here is a practical hardware-to-model mapping table for local, quantized inference (4-bit unless otherwise noted). These ranges assume modern inference engines (llama.cpp, vLLM, TensorRT-LLM, etc.) and reasonable context windows (4k–8k). Real performance varies by model architecture and tuning.

Hardware Usable VRAM / Unified Memory Max Model Size (Quantized) Typical Tokens/sec Ideal Use Case

MacBook M3 (16–24GB) 16–24GB unified 7B – 13B 15–40 t/s Portable personal assistant, writing, light coding

MacBook M3 Pro (36–48GB) 36–48GB unified 30B 10–25 t/s Research, heavier RAG, advanced local workflows

MacBook M3 Max (64GB) 64GB unified 70B 8–18 t/s Full private knowledge assistant, serious reasoning

MacBook M3 Max (128GB) 128GB unified 70B – 120B 6–15 t/s High-end sovereign "AI brain" with large context + RAG

RTX 3060 (12GB) 12GB VRAM 7B – 13B 25–40 t/s Budget local LLM, experimentation

RTX 4070 (12GB) 12GB VRAM 13B 30–45 t/s Fast personal assistant, light coding

RTX 3090 (24GB) 24GB VRAM 14B – 30B 40–80 t/s (7B) Developer workstation, RAG, fine-tuning (LoRA)

RTX 4090 (24GB) 24GB VRAM 14B – 30B 50–100 t/s (7B) Fast local coding, creative writing, agent workflows

Dual RTX 3090 (48GB total) 48GB VRAM 70B 18–30 t/s Enterprise-grade private LLM, internal copilots

Dual RTX 4090 (48GB total) 48GB VRAM 70B (headroom) 22–35 t/s Small org inference server, multi-user workload

RTX 6000 Ada (48GB) 48GB VRAM 70B (single GPU) 25–40 t/s Professional deployment, reliability-focused

A100 40GB 40GB VRAM 70B (4-bit) 25–35 t/s Production inference node

A100 80GB 80GB VRAM 70B (8-bit) 40–65 t/s Enterprise backend, heavier batching

H100 80GB 80GB VRAM 70B – 120B (MoE or optimized) 60–90+ t/s High-throughput production inference

Interpretation notes:

For 7B–13B models, nearly any modern GPU with 12GB VRAM is sufficient at 4-bit quantization. These models are extremely responsive and excellent for personal copilots, note drafting, summarization, and light RAG.

For 30B-class models, 24GB VRAM (3090/4090) is the practical sweet spot. This tier feels dramatically more capable for structured reasoning, code generation, and long-form synthesis while remaining fast.

For 70B-class models, 48GB total VRAM (dual GPUs or high-memory workstation cards) becomes the sovereignty threshold. This tier approximates "frontier-like" reasoning for private deployments. It is ideal for enterprise copilots and serious internal knowledge systems.

Above 70B, you enter diminishing returns relative to hardware cost unless you are serving many users or need very high reasoning density. At that point, enterprise accelerators (A100/H100) make more sense than consumer cards.

Mac unified memory systems (64–128GB) are unique because they blur CPU/GPU memory boundaries. While raw throughput may be lower than multi-GPU NVIDIA setups, they allow surprisingly large models in a single portable machine, making them compelling for high-end personal sovereign deployments.

General rules:

4-bit quantization is what makes 30B and 70B models realistic on workstation hardware. KV cache size grows with context window; very long context reduces effective throughput. RAG often provides more practical benefit than jumping to a larger base model.

Hardware determines your sovereignty ceiling.

7B–13B = personal productivity.

30B = serious developer-grade reasoning.

70B = organizational intelligence node.
Datacenter GPUs = multi-user production infrastructure.

www.ingramcontent.com/pod-product-compliance
Lightning Source LLC
LaVergne TN
LVHW101616210926
848480LV00009B/644

* 9 7 9 8 2 3 3 3 5 0 4 4 3 *